THE BOOK OF MARLOW

FRONT COVER : An early 19th century print of The Royal Military College cadets on parade before George III (right of the hatless officer in the right foreground), at Remnantz, Marlow—since much changed and without the wooden temporary buildings, probably barracks. The parade ground is now a field. (By permission of Cdr O. F. M. Wethered, RN, DL, JP.)

The church and bridge from an artist's impression published 1797, showing the first bridge, eel baskets and cattle watering in the centre of the town. (Marlow Library).

THE BOOK OF MARLOW

AN ILLUSTRATED RECORD

BY

A. J. (Jock) CAIRNS

BARRACUDA BOOKS LIMITED
CHESHAM, BUCKINGHAMSHIRE, ENGLAND
MCMLXXVI

PUBLISHED BY BARRACUDA BOOKS LIMITED

CHESHAM, ENGLAND

AND PRINTED BY

MALCOLM G. READ LIMITED

175 BERMONDSEY STREET

LONDON SE 1

BOUND BY

BOOKBINDERS OF LONDON LIMITED

LONDON N5

JACKET PRINTED BY

WHITE CRESCENT PRESS LIMITED

LUTON, ENGLAND

LITHOGRAPHY BY

SOUTH MIDLANDS LITHO PLATES LIMITED

LUTON, ENGLAND

TYPE SET IN

MONOTYPE BASKERVILLE SERIES 169

BY SOUTH BUCKS TYPESETTERS LIMITED

BEACONSFIELD, ENGLAND

ISBN 0 86023 017 1

Contents

Acknowledgements

Much is owed to many in the way of thanks to bring about The Book of Marlow. I am grateful to many old-established Marlow families for providing a great many hitherto unpublished illustrations; also to all those people who gave me information, advice and encouragement in this task.

Principally, I am most grateful to my colleague of many years' standing, Clive Birch, who originally made the approach to me about writing this book. Clive, apart from being tolerant with me during two quite painful illnesses has been my inspiration, my mentor— and at times, my tormentor. But I hope that the passage of time will show that Marlow owes a greater debt to him than to me for making possible the first illustrated volume on the history of the town of Marlow and its environs.

My thanks are due to many other people scattered over a wide area. To Mr Christopher Gowing of the Bucks County Museum and to Miss Rosemary Ewles, a member of his staff for her considerable assistance in arranging photographs; to Mr Leslie Cram of the Reading Museum and Art Gallery; to Mr Brian Forbes of Aerofilms at Elstree; the Director of the County Records Office, and Miss Stark in the archives department; to Mr Arthur Church, Editor of The Bucks Free Press for his support and encouragement and the 'Free Press' archivist Mrs Elizabeth Smith; and to Miss Purser of Marlow Library branch for her help in the handling of the subscriptions as well as providing useful advice. Also to Mr John Sansom of The Marlow Bookshelf for his assistance with the subscriptions.

I am indebted to another friend of many years, Alan Holmes, as almost all photographic reproductions are the results of his professional eye for detail and meticulous work in the darkroom; and to John Armistead for further photographic work.

Formal acknowledgements are also due to the Public Record Office for reproductions of Crown copyright material by permission of the Controller of HM Stationery Office and the Mansell Collection.

My personal thanks for permission to reproduce the magnificent front cover go to Commander Owen Wethered, to whom I am also indebted for writing the foreword.

Without the backing of friends like Mr Jim Tonge, Mrs E. A. B. Orr of Marlow Society, Mr Gerry Lake, Councillor John Hester and the late Councillor Frank Edmonds this work would be that much poorer for they provided the bulk of the illustrations, with a further ready response from Mr John Allen, Mr Frederick Keeley and Mr Reg Sparks, to whom I am also grateful.

STATION APPROACH,
MARLOW
January 1976.

Foreword

by Commander O. F. M. Wethered, RN, DL, JP

In writing The Book of Marlow Mr A. J. Cairns set himself a mammoth task and, in fact, he begins his story at the time when mammoths roamed the country. This book is no ordinary guide to a town and the writer has delved deeply and thoroughly into the events which brought Marlow into being. The enquiring mind of the journalist has stood him in good stead and, having dealt with its history, Mr Cairns describes in interesting detail the life led by Marlow citizens from the beginning to present times. His accounts of the town's activities are both interesting and instructive, covering as they do a very wide field. The author and those who have helped to compile this book are to be congratulated and I am glad to have had the opportunity of contributing this short foreword.

REMNANTZ,
MARLOW.
January 1976.

Preface

by the Town Mayor of Marlow

Apart from a short history of the town of Marlow written by the late Mr J. C. Davies in 1962, no history devoted entirely to the town has ever been attempted. Mr Davies's work, produced on behalf of the Marlow Society, was not illustrated.

I therefore congratulate the publishers and Jock Cairns for endeavouring to do something which has been long overdue, namely producing a comprehensive and illustrated account of Marlow since its beginning.

I understand the author has had to travel far and wide in order to research his material. It seems unfortunate that there is no central reference department in Marlow where documents and artifacts could be displayed publicly on a permanent basis. Such a place would be of great benefit to the education of succeeding generations and would also add considerable interest to visitors to the town and stimulate Marlow's tourist image.

COURT GARDEN,
MARLOW.
January 1976.

Fayre Quarry Wood

'Lone in my boat I'm wont to dream
Upon the beauty of this stream.
How joyously did Nature smile
Upon this heart of temp'rate isle.
No greater painter ever could
Improve upon fayre Quarry Wood,
Where bluebirds trill for all they're worth,
This be the fayrest place on earth.'

(Anon), 1866.

This poem was discovered by Mr Henry Clayton in his great-grandfather's diary.

Dedication

For the People of Marlow to whom I owe so much in kindness and friendship.

Man and Marlow

It has taken 4,500 million years to shape Marlow. Within that mind-numbing time-scale Man's existence on the planet Earth is less than the flicker of an eyelid—a mere 1,750,000 years. Yet Man has survived, developing through several sub-species until he emerged as he is now.

Armed only with insatiable curiosity, unbelievable tenacity of purpose and infinite adaptability he has moulded successive environments to his needs or has been expedient when his survival was threatened.

To appreciate how he has overcome the awe-inspiring elements, the mind has to be projected almost to the threshold of time itself.

Even then, much of what may be visualised in this conjecture is no more than speculation. Scientists have argued, and will continue to wrangle over the evolution both of earth and of man.

The only certain thing is that everything that did happen from the beginning to the present day was destined to have some bearing on the formation of Marlow's place in the world.

This is that story.

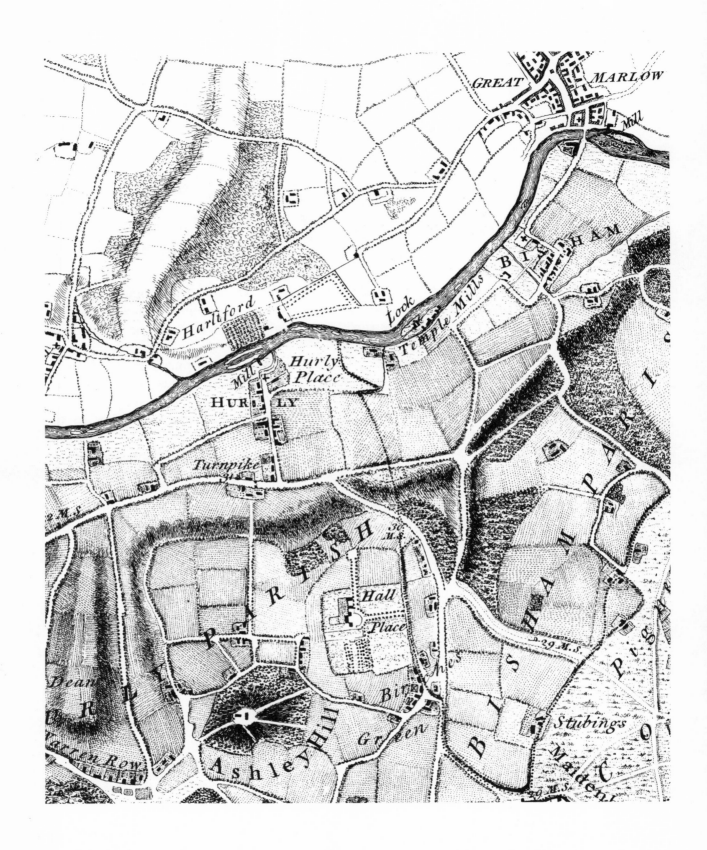

'Great Marlow, Harliford and Medmenham', as they were in 1761.

Merlaw

Sharks swam over Marlow ground seventy million years ago. Two million years back mammoths and woolly rhinoceros wandered around the barren tundra lands left in the wake of the Ice Age. The teeth, tusks and bones they left behind are the proof.

Not far away dinosaurs roamed the lower foothills of the Chilterns and the Vale of Aylesbury where at least one of them laid down to die. A million years ago the tundra began to be clothed in richer vegetation. Forests approaching jungle proportions replaced the wide open spaces. Then came man.

His courage was never wanting, but once there was a time when he was faced with an almost insurmountable barrier. When the Chalk Sea receded—this was how the shark became trapped—there were peaks of land etching the skyline, just as they do today, 500 feet above the enormous lake of water separating the north and south of the valley that was to become Marlow. For centuries this vast area of water was to prove both a barrier and a highway to the first ones.

Long before events and historical facts were recorded our ancestors must have gazed out from their cave dwellings in the Quarry Woods and Winter Hill, screwing up courage to face the unknown water element in order to satisfy their curiosity as to what lay deep within the forests to the north and on the escarpment rolling away towards the sunset. Time passed and the strangers arrived.

Elephants still roamed the Thames Valley, a quarter of a million years ago, when man first arrived. The river changed its level over the next two hundred and forty thousand years. It was during that time that Early Stone Age man first visited Marlow, leaving his flint implements behind there and at Medmenham. Perhaps he found the water too great a barrier, for his successors in the Middle Stone Age left no evidence of their passing, but some five thousand years later New Stone Age families must have settled the valley, for their cooking pots, celts (tools), and their hunting arrows have since proved these were the first farmers in the area.

Those first communities would have settled in downlike areas, near the escarpment, grazing the hillsides. Their successors of the Bronze Age c. 1800 BC, used the water for transport, and at Marlow and Bourne End they established substantial settlements—their ornaments, coins and craft have survived the centuries. At Danesfield Ditches, not far away, Bronze Age man dropped a spear and made his indelible mark on the terrain with an entrenchment.

By the Iron Age, some 400 years BC, South Bucks was relatively densely populated, and a series of fortifications established along the Chilterns. Danesfield Ditches became one of these encampments, and the early route from Oxfordshire to Bourne End established in the Bronze Age, was now in regular use. Iron Age man left behind pottery—and the first evidence of local trade in the shape of a gold coin.

However, South Bucks was virtually still an island region when the Romans arrived first in 55 BC, flanked by the broad waters of the Thames, and as a result Marlow lay somewhat off the mainstream of national events. If the Romans came, they saw and went again, leaving nothing except a 4th century coin to mark their passage.

When the Romans came over, they brought mercenaries from the Teutonic races of the Continent. Some of these peoples stayed and by the time the Jutes invaded Kent and the Isle of Wight, their cousins were already settled and intermingled with the original natives.

During these times seven kingdoms were formed and Marlow ended up as a southern outpost of Mercia. The Saxons were now much in evidence and, good watermen as they were, they could not have been impressed by Marlow's huge lake.

It was they who began to drain it. The Normans finished the job and found, when they came to compile the Domesday Book, that the area had been named by these primitive engineers.

They had dubbed the district 'Merlaw'. In Anglo-Saxon this simply means: 'What is left after draining a mere'.

The Manor of Merlaw was held by Algar, the Earl of Mercia. After the Norman Conquest, King William took it from his son, and as Thomas Langley wrote: 'bestowed it upon Queen Matilda'.

By the time Queen Matilda, wife of the Conqueror, owned Marlow, there were two mills drawing power from the river and providing incomes, and the eels from the river were another important source of profit—1500 of them were caught each year.

The mammoth roamed Marlow two million years ago—this was his tooth (five inches long). (Reading Museum and Art Gallery).

ABOVE: A mammoth also left his tusk behind at Marlow. (Behind this is part of one of his contemporaries, a woolly rhinoceros). (Bucks County Museum).

ABOVE RIGHT: Seventy million years ago, sharks swam in the seas that covered Little Marlow—this is a surviving tooth. (Bucks County Museum).

BELOW: Stone Age Man used these flints as tools and axes, and left them behind in Marlow. (Bucks County Museum).

ABOVE: This Belgic urn was in use in Quarry Woods
in the Bronze Age. (Reading Museum & Art Gallery).

LEFT: Bronze Age man dropped these spearheads in the
Thames at Marlow. (Bucks County Museum)

BELOW: A Roman soldier or trader mislaid this Constantine
(330-350 AD) coin in local waters. (Bucks County Museum).

16

In the Royal Manor

Before the Norman Conquest Marlow and the neighbouring district were divided up into a number of manorial holdings, principally Great Marlow, Little Marlow, and Medmenham. England's Queen Edith held Little Marlow, and after the Conquest when the new king's wife Matilda owned Great Marlow, truly the Marlows were royal territory.

As the various holdings changed hands, through inheritance, marriage, gift, purchase or outright force, they gradually merged and the principal landowning families emerged.

The translation of Marlow's entry in the Domesday Book reads: 'Queen Matilda holds Merlave which is taxed for 15 hides. There are 26 plough lands. In demesne 5 hides, and there are two ploughs & 35 villeins with 23 copyholders have 24 ploughs. There is one servant and a mill worth 20s. There are 26 carucates of pasture. The woods supply pannage for 1000 hogs, and a fishery which produces 1000 eels. For all dues it is worth 25l. when the queen received it 10l. and as much in the reign of Edward the confessor when earl Algar held it'.

So far no one has ever spelled out where Marlow's manor house stood. References are made to Harleyford Manor house; the manor at Seymours, presumably Seymour Court which was alleged to be the birthplace of Jane Seymour, though no documentary evidence exists to back this; there is a mention of the manor at Widmer (now Widmere Farm).

J. C. Davies, history master at Sir William Borlase's School for many years, speculated on this. In his view the Manor must have been somewhere near Town Farm, just off Henley Road. But in 1542 Tucher Bold, lord of the manor of Harleyford, obtained permission to have a priest at his house at Harleyford. That house was set on fire in the 1580's and by 1640 Lord Paget lived in what was known as the manor house. This house was damaged in the Civil War (as was Seymour Court), and pulled down in 1755, to be replaced by the present building.

Today the Lord of the Manor is Sir Arthur Clayton, DSC, the 11th baronet. The family of de Claytone entered England with William the Norman, Roger de Claytone being the standard bearer to the Conqueror. He shared prodigally in the plunder.

It was not until 1716 that the family became connected with the manor of Marlow. William Clayton built Harleyford, became president of Guy's Hospital, London and in 1732 was made a baronet. His uncle, William Clayton, rode into London in 1660 at the Restoration of the Monarchy. In 1679 he was proclaimed Lord Mayor of London and in 1688 joined the call to bring the Prince of Orange to these shores. He died at his estate at Marden Park, Surrey in 1707, and having no children bequeathed his property to William, his nephew, who became Lord of the Manor at Marlow.

The first baronet had two sons and the younger, William, became MP for Bucks. The fourth baronet in 1799, Sir William Robert Clayton, had five sons. The eldest, William fought at Waterloo and he became MP for Marlow in 1832.

Two years later he became the fifth baronet on the death of his father. By this time he had attained the rank of General. He was succeeded in 1866 by his 24-year-old grandson Sir William Clayton. He married Aimee MacKenzie of Fawley Court and ruled his squiredom for 58 years during which time he became High Sheriff of Buckinghamshire.

He died in 1914 without issue and the baronetcy devolved on the descendants of the second son of General Clayton-East. East had two sons, Gilbert and Augustus Henry. Sir Gilbert inherited the baronetcy in 1914. His son George became the eighth baronet in 1925 but died after only six months.

Sir George's son, Robert, aged 18, became ninth baronet of Marden and fifth baronet of Hall Place. He assumed by deed the additional surname of Clayton after that of Clayton East.

In 1932 he married Dorothy Durrant, and they were acclaimed as England's most handsome couple—and the happiest. After only six months Sir Robert died and the line of Clayton Easts suddenly became extinct. Less than a year later his young widow died in an aircraft crash.

The baronetcy of Marden now devolved upon the Augustus Clayton branch of the family. The son of the Reverend Augustus was Fitzroy. He married Lady Isabel Taylour, the daughter of the Marquis of Headfort. He was knighted, became president of the Royal National Lifeboat Institution and lived at Fyfield House, Maidenhead.

His younger son, Cecil, married Kathleen Bradish-Ellames of The Manor House, Little Marlow. His eldest son, Harold, married Leila Clayton. In 1932 he inherited the baronetcy from Sir Robert. His son, Sir Arthur Harold Dudley Clayton, became the 11th baronet in 1951, and remains Lord of the Manor of Marlow.

Harleyford estate was handed over as a recreational area for the people, stipulating that the grounds should never be built on. The grounds are laid out for a caravan park and there is a marina on the Thames.

While speculation has failed to prove the existence, let alone the whereabouts of Marlow's original manor house, as the manor itself was merely a series of rights and obligations over territory and inhabitants, this is not surprising, for the Queen could hardly live in all her manors.

Marlow, or Great Marlow Manor as it then was, comprised some 15 hides (1,800 acres measured in economic rather than territorial terms), in the early 11th century. As Crown land, forming part of the Honour of Gloucester, it fell to the Earl of Gloucester in 1121.

The Gloucesters held the manor until 1326 when Hugh le Dispenseur was hanged, and his widow, retaining Marlow, married a Mortimer. Despite this, Marlow stayed within the Dispenseur family until the lands passed to a sister Isabel, wife of Richard Beauchamp, Earl of Warwick, and she settled the manor in 1439 on her son, Henry, later Duke of Warwick. His sister inherited and retained Marlow until 1515 when a 21-year lease granted the manor to Tucher Bold. The Bolds held the lease for a further period until 1554 when they conveyed their interest to William, Lord Paget of Beauchamp. This raised something of a furore as the Daunays, who held a mortgage on the land, brought an action. This was settled and then challenged, but the Pagets were still in possession in 1628. Thereafter it passed through the hands of the Moores, Sir Humphrey Winch, Bt, Lord Falkland and Sir James Etheridge—both MPs for Marlow in the 17/18th centuries.

In 1719 Sir John Guise, another Marlow MP, acquired the manor, which passed to his son in 1732—but Guise, obeying his father's will, alienated the manor in 1735 to Sir William Clayton, Bt.

Little Marlow comprised some 600 acres. Though the Bishop of Bayeux acquired the manor on the Conquest redistribution of England's lands, the Gloucesters took over when Odo fell from grace, but they appear to have virtually handed the estate over intact to the priory until the dissolution, when Bisham Abbey acquired the property. This change lasted but one year when Little Marlow passed into the hands first of John Tytley and Elizabeth Restwold, then John Lord Williams of Thame, and subsequently five Wilmots, one of whom alienated his rights to William Bury who conveyed it to John Borlase in 1561. At this point the Crown intervened, and laying claim by way of a grant made to Anne of Cleves in 1541, sought to take over. But Borlase hung on, and by his death in 1593 had put together the five separated portions. The family retained the manor, until in 1781 it was sold to Gen Sir George Nugent, Bt, to pay Admiral Sir John Borlase Warren's debts. The Ellames acquired the estate in 1862.

The Marlows included other manors—Harleyford, Widmere, Seymours and Bormer in Great Marlow, and Danvers, Losemere, Monkton in Little Marlow.

Harleyford may have been so named as it lay opposite Hurley (Hurley ford). It was small—only 120 acres in value at Domesday—and granted by Gloucester to one William Pincerna, in the 12th century. By 1269 it had passed to the de Harleyfords, but they died out and in 1464 John Flegg purchased the tenure, and it became known as Harleyford Manor. After passing through various hands, mainly by marriage and inheritance, the estate came to Tucher Bold in 1536, and in 1571 it was still in the Bolds' possession. The manor house which was set on fire while Richard Bold was away in the Low Countries, then became the centre of interest, for the Privy Council summoned a man called Heywood in 1586/7 for this act of arson, which had caused 1,000 marks' worth of damage. Ten years later the manor was conveyed to Miles Hobart, a citizen of London, whose son inherited, was knighted and sat as Marlow's MP in 1627-8. On March 2, 1629 he locked the door of the House, pocketed the key but found himself in the Tower until 1631, to be released for a few months before his coach overturned on Holborn Hill, killing him.

Hobart's heirs, John Rous and Margaret Holborne, divided the manor, but both portions were bought by William King and Ralph Chase, which led to disputes as Margaret's father had been attainted for piracy in 1592, and in 1640 it was claimed that her part was in the hands of the Crown's representative, Lord Paget. Paget finally acquired the estate and the manor house formed the link with Great Marlow, as the lord's chief residence for both estates, thenceforth joined. It figured in the Civil War, was pulled down in 1755 and replaced by today's building a year later—to be immortalized by Kenneth Grahame as Toad Hall.

Widmere Manor's origins are uncertain, but Godric, a man of Asgar the Staller, held about 750 acres in Saxon times, and by the time of Domesday (1086) the estate belonged to Walter de Vernon. By 1248 the Knights Hospitallers were in possession, but in 1254 the Knights Templars laid claim to it. The lands were variously leased until 1541 when they were acquired by John Lord Russell, the Russells passing it over to Sir William Borlase in 1623. Sixty-four years later Borlase relatives, the Grenvilles sold the estate to William Clayton and from 1799 Widmere was amalgamated with Great Marlow.

Seymours was held by Mulcheney Abbey, Somerset, until the dissolution, when it was bestowed on Edward Seymour, Earl of Hertford, who concluded a deal with the Crown, following which the lands went to Bristol Cathedral. The lease held from the dean and chapter by John Seamer (Seymour) of Marlow originated in 1541 and was confirmed in 1549; on his death in 1567 the churchwardens laid claim to vestments of cloth of gold they said were entrusted to him, and which it was claimed had been sold to him by Edward VI's commissioners. Seymour left the farm to his widow, appointing his cook, Hugh Dawson executor, with a claim to the estate if his widow died or remarried during the period of the lease. Dawson acquired Seymours and left it to his widow. The farm passed through several hands by legacy until in 1633 the dean and chapter granted two leases to the Powis family, who despite debts and sequestration retained them until 1748, when they were sold. The freehold was acquired by Thomas Owen Wethered of Remnantz in 1862.

Barmoor, or Bormer Manor was formed in the 13th century from Gloucester's holdings; it included three mills known as Gosenham Mills. (One is sometimes called Harleyford Mill.)

A substantial Saxon holding at Little Marlow, consisting of over a thousand acres was in the hands of Haming, one of King Edward's thegns until Miles Crispin absorbed it on the Conquest. Ralf and Roger, thought to be the sons of Roland de Anvers who rode with William of Normandy in 1066, became Crispin's tenants. Ralf's share became Danvers; Roger's became Losemere.

Danvers Manor stayed in Ralf's family until the 14th century. A Danvers was patron of Little Marlow Priory. The following century the Ingoldsby's were in possession, until in 1536 Sir John Baldwin, chief justice of Common Pleas took possession and his grandson John Borlase joined it with Little Marlow Manor.

Losemere descended through the Beauchamps, Ramsays and Clarkes until 1660, thereafter passing into other hands, until the Chase family acquired Westhorpe House and held the estate into the late 18th century. At the end of that century Nugent bought house and land.

Monkton Manor was so called from the 16th century, owned as it was by the Abbot and monks of Medmenham. In 1540 Monkton was granted to goldsmith John Chaundler, and he and Robert Traps alienated it to justice Baldwin. The manorial tenant William Lovejoy promptly sued Chaundler and Traps for breach of contract, claiming he had financed the purchase of the manor from the Crown, but he failed and the manor passed down the Baldwin line to the Borlases and was joined with Little Marlow.

Crawlton's Manor belonged to Bisham Abbey, but in 1537 passed to Chaundler and thence to Borlase. His claim was contested by the Crown as part of the dispute arising from the earlier 1541 connection with Anne of Cleves, but Chaundler's original 1540 grant was upheld. Crawltons was also joined with Little Marlow.

Medmenham Manor, which was eventually joined with Little Marlow until the mid 19th century, was held by Wulstan, one of King Edward's thegns. The Conquest saw the Saxon noble replaced by the powerful Hugh de Bolebec, whose family became Earls of Oxford. The estate passed through marriage to the Earls of Surrey, the Earl of Arundel, and other noble holders until in 1553 it was granted by Queen Mary to the Rice family. William Borlase bought the manor in 1595.

Part of the manor went in 1415 to the Duchess of Norfolk, and in 1506 that estate reverted to the Crown. It probably included the Bolebec castle, known as Bulbek Manor in 1539—in 1771 there were local references to Bullbank's Castle. The rights included fisheries (for eels) and mills.

The Norman surveyors catalogued Marlow for posterity in the Domesday
Book, 1086. (By permission of The Controller of
Her Majesty's Stationery Office.)

ABOVE: Queen Matilda's lands at Great Marlow.   CENTRE RIGHT: Widmer Manor.

CENTRE LEFT: Danvers and Losemere—one 1086 holding.   BELOW: The Manor of Little Marlow.

21

ABOVE: The original Harleyford manor house seen from upstream (behind the boat), with Danesfield chapel on the skyline.

BELOW: 18th century downstream view of Marlow.

To the Memory of
SIR WILLIAM ROBERT CLAYTON, BART.
of Harleyford, in the County of Bucks.
Born 2nd August 1842.
Departed this life 7th October 1914.

*This Tablet
is erected by his Wife.*

ABOVE LEFT: Harleyford manor house as it is today—rebuilt 1715 by the
first baronet of Marden, Sir William Clayton.

RIGHT: Sir William Clayton, father of Harleyford's first Clayton lord,
and Lord Mayor of London, 1679—in the grounds of Harleyford.

BELOW LEFT: Longest serving Harleyford lord, Sir William
Robert Clayton was sixth baronet of Marden—
remembered in Marlow Parish Church.

ABOVE CENTRE: Little Marlow

CENTRE: The lands

BELOW CENTRE: Seymou
birthplace of Jane S

LEFT AND RIGHT: The armoria
Clare, Despenser; centre left: Bo
above right: Beauchamp, Ne
Below righ

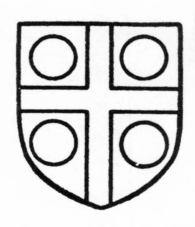

—extended over the centuries.

wned at Marlow.

gendary, but unproven,
e to Henry VIII.

f Marlow's lords. Above left:
below left: Borlase, Warren;
right: Clayton, Nugent;
anvers.

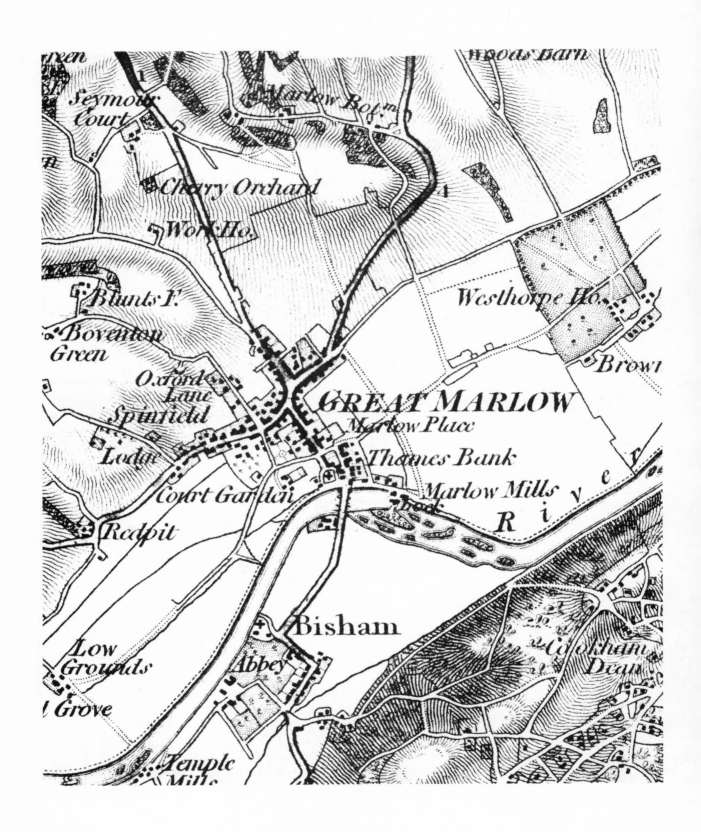

This 18th century map shows the growing network of local
communications. (Marlow Library).

By Wheel and by Wharf

The earliest forms of transport in the Marlow area were water-borne. But as time went by, carts and chariots rolled along the uplands overlooking the valley and the lake.

It is significant that the Roman road engineers gave the district a wide berth. They devoted their attentions to the old Bath Road south of the river and used the ancient Icknield Way to the north. But they navigated the water. Any Roman relics have been found either in or close to the river, bearing further witness to their disinterest in local land, densely cloaked by forest.

After the Roman Legions pulled back there was still a reluctance on the part of their successors, to use the muddy, water-logged valley floor for travelling.

Thousands of feet and hooves beat out the well-marked paths high up in the Chilterns and it was along these tracks that the Saxons of Marlow traded and warred with their Celtic neighbours over the hills in Wycombe. And so for many centuries these tracks and the Thames were to provide the only life-lines.

After the Norman Conquest the Domesday Book described 'Widmer' (now Widmere) Manor: 'Ralf and Roger hold of Milo Crispin in Merlawe 8 hides and an half and half a yard land. There are six plough lands: in demesne two, and fourteen villeins with six copy-holders have four plough lands. There are two servants—six carucates of pasture, wood for 200 hogs, and 12d rent. For all dues it is worth 60 shillings: in the reign of Edward the Confessor 41. when Haming, a thane of the king's, held it, and had the power of selling it'.

Milo Crispin died in 1107 without any issue and his lands then went to the crown. As a result the Manor was granted to the Knights Hospitallers, and then the Knights Templars and it was this which brought about the first great leap forward in local communications.

Part-soldiers, part-monks the Knights Templars already had a settlement at Bisham. Ultimately granted Widmere, they needed access between the two establishments and it appears likely that it was the members of this Order who first threw the spans of a bridge across the river Thames, even though other manors held the rights to the ferries that had sufficed until then.

The route ran from what was at one time known as Duck Lane, because there was a ducking stool by the riverside, now St Peter Street across the river to what is now the 'Compleat Angler' hotel gardens, ultimately connecting Wycombe and Reading.

Thus, the final barrier was broken down and from then on the settlement that was to become Marlow began to take shape on the northern bank of the Thames.

There is evidence that Merlaw was renamed soon after the erection of the bridge. Now Chipping-Marlow existed and thrived. The word 'Chipping' indicates that a market was held, and the landowners built private wharves along the banks.

A market would inevitably attract people and those with things to sell would transport them as best they could in the early carts and waggons. With access to the south bank, local agriculture prospered.

A timber-built boat from the Bronze Age was recovered from the river in 1871. A crude

27

vessel this, but it had been effective in its day. Now the craft that began to appear in increasing numbers were the forerunners of the barges and narrow boats to come.

Regulating the river was much in mind in 1695 when Stephen and James Chase, Edmund Waller and Henry Gould went to Marlow Lock to set 'two spikes of iron' to mark the level of the flash locks. The mark was confirmed at a special court sitting at the Three Tuns on August 27.

Timber, wool and grain were loaded on to the barges at Port Marlow, a wharf at the bottom of St Peter Street. Minerals dredged from the river bed and loaded into barges were disgorged at the same wharf. And supplementing the commerce on water were trains of pack-horses and mules and donkeys.

The routes taken by these animal trains were varied but it is significant that by the 18th century they were able to move with ease along the banks of the river Thames. Gone were the forests and undergrowth that made the Romans balk. The farmers and nesters had edged into the trees to recover the good, fertile earth to bring it under the command of man.

One of these routes ran between Bourne End and Marlow. So when in 1872 the Great Marlow Railway Company came into being it was not unnatural that the pawky Marlow humour should christen the new iron horse, 'The Marlow Donkey'. And the name stuck to the mule-train successor. Even today the diesel-driven, one, two or three coached train is still referred to as 'The Donkey'. Despite the introduction of power for transport on rail, road transport still relied on horses as the motive force.

In the late 18th and early 19th centuries 'The Marlow Flier' left High Street on its twice daily journey to Piccadilly, London—a trip lasting three hours. The 'Flier' was based at the 'Crown' inn, a coaching house where Lloyds Bank now stands, but a building that has nothing to do with the 'Crown' of today.

In 1888, William Wickens provided a waggon service twice a week from Horns, Chapel street to the New Inn near the Old Bailey, returning two days later, and John Day was his sole competitor with a twice weekly service. John Palmer provided a weekly service to Reading, and likewise to Wycombe.

Though by present day standards the surfacing of the roads was poor, they had come a long way from the tracks that greeted Daniel Defoe when he visited Marlow around the mid-1720s.

'Marlow is a town of great embarkation on the Thames, not so much for goods wrought here (for the trade of the town is chiefly in bone lace) but for the goods from the neighbouring towns, and particularly a very great quantity of malt and meal is brought hither from High Wickham.'

'Between High Wickham and Marlow is a little river called the Loddon (Wye?) on which are a great many mills, and particularly corn mills and paper mills; the first of these grind and dress the wheat and the meal is sent to Marlow and loaded on board barges for London; and the second makes great quantities of printing paper and that very good of its kind and cheap, such as is generally made use of in printing our newspapers, journals etc., and smaller pamphlets; but not much fine or large for bound books or writing.

'On the river of Thames, just by the side of this town, though on the other bank, are three very remarkable mills, which are called the Temple Mills and are also called the Brass Mills and are for making Bisham Abbey Battery work, as they call it, viz. brass kettles and pans of all sorts.

'Next to these are two mills, both extraordinary in themselves, one for making thimbles, a work excellently well finished and which performs to admiration, and another for pressing of oil from rape seed and flax seed both which as I was told turn to very good account to the proprietors. Here is also brought down a vast quantity of beech wood which grows in the woods of Buckinghamshire more plentifully than in any other part of England. This is the most useful wood for some uses that grows, and without which the City of London would be put to more difficulty than for anything of its kind in the nation.'

The postal service was somewhat different in 1888: three deliveries and four despatches daily from West street under postmaster Charlton Butler; twice daily collections and despatches at Little Marlow for posting through Great Marlow Post Office, with Henry Valentine Hussey in charge.

By the end of the 19th century transportation began to take on a new form with the coming of the early steam-lorries and first of the petrol engined wagons. The trickle of engined vehicles was to become a flood bringing in its wake countless problems for the road designers and engineers. Not the least of these headaches was the crossing of the river.

Earlier, Thomas Langley had inspected records in the Tower, now moved to the Public Records Office; patent rolls granted by Edward III, Richard II and Henry IV to allow the bailiffs to take toll of all goods, wares, merchandize and cattle passing over or under the bridge. The money collected by the bailiffs was then to be used to keep the bridge in a state of repair. The earliest surviving reference to cash for repairs dates as far back as 1294, and John de Waltinton was warden in 1227. The last two Royal grants record that the bailiffs appointed to receive the tolls were the Prior of Bisham, John Seemere, Nicholas Monkton and John Blunt.

Bad times lay ahead for royalty, though, and after King Charles I was beheaded and the country was thrown into a state of Civil War, the old Marlow Bridge became a casualty. No actual account of how or why the bridge was damaged can be traced, though the bridge was damaged when it was pulled up by soldiers in the army of Maj Gen Brown in 1644.

Whether this was a tactical or strategic move as part of military necessity or just a wanton act of vandalism may never now be established, but the damage to the bridge was looked upon as a serious matter even by Parliament itself from whom a warrant was issued to levy a county rate for its repair.

Obviously the bridge must have been repaired at that time, but the structure burst on the scene again quite dramatically in 1787. It was described then as having become 'very ruinous and unsafe'.

An application was made to the county in that year for it to be rebuilt. There was an immediate wrangle from the authorities, the magistrates not being entirely satisfied that the bridge was a county responsibility. They indicated there was an estate of 20l. per annum belonging to the bridge, and this was vested in bridge-wardens who were appointed by the inhabitants. The request was denied.

To the rescue came the then Marquis of Buckingham who sponsored a public subscription for the bridge's replacement. In 1789—two years after the description of the structure would have led anyone to believe it was ready to fall down—the subscription raised 18,001.

Langley records: 'A handsome wooden bridge was built, which is very commodious, much improves the avenues of the town, and is a pleasing object to the surrounding country.'

Almost certainly the new bridge was constructed on the site of the old, for within a mere 40 years yet a third bridge was to become the centre of controversy—and surely few bridges in the world have ever given rise to such widely varying viewpoints as the third structure to span the Thames linking Buckinghamshire to Berkshire at Marlow.

At a cost of £22,000 including the approaches to it and the costs of the necessary Act of

Parliament, Marlow's world renowned suspension bridge was strung over the Thames. It took three years to complete between 1829 and 1832.

Suspension bridges were fashionable at that time and Telford's influence was still strong. The man who supervised the construction of the iron chains, reaching out over the water to the two stone built towers on the banks was John Tierney Clark.

Who could have foreseen a fully laden tank transporter making an attempt to cross almost 120 years later? No doubt Tierney Clark would not have been surprised that his structure still stood after such a load had successfully negotiated the crossing, but the experience proved too much for the bridge and a five tons weight restriction was introduced and rigidly imposed.

This threw commercial traffic into all sorts of chaos. The nearest crossings were seven miles downstream to Cookham or a similar distance upstream to Henley. Worse was to follow. Following a thorough inspection in 1960, engineers declared the bridge to be unsafe for anything more than two tons.

Then began the most epoch-making wrangle of all.

It was around 1932 that an inspection was made of the area by surveyors. Architects and planners drew lines on maps and declared that Marlow would have a by-pass.

In 1939 the population of the town was still waiting with baited breath for final news of their relief road, but the wailing sirens of Sunday, 3rd September 1939, heralded the death knell of those hopes. At the same time, it was perhaps a fortuitous disappointment.

Few people in 1939 could have visualised the tremendous strides to be made in the years up to 1945. At the end of hostilities vehicles 30 years ahead of their time thundered along roads that were 30 years behind the times—and to make matters worse, sadly neglected at that.

It seems remarkable to recall that in 1949 in high summer, trees formed an almost perfect arch all the way up the main road to High Wycombe from Marlow Bottom to Burroughs Grove and there was barely room for a 'bus and lorry to pass on the metalled surface—what there was of it. A similar situation prevailed at Wooburn on the Holtspur Road until 1958. And even in 1975 such conditions exist on the main Marlow to Maidenhead highway.

So in 1946 the people of Marlow began to suffer the first pangs of traffic congestion. As more cars became available to the individual the town centre was one seething mass of moving metal, and not always moving metal.

The cry was taken up again in those early post-war years for Marlow to be by-passed. Nothing was seen to be done. But the draughtsmen dusted off their plans of 1932 and began to take another look, prodded in their labours by persistent complaints from traffic troubled Marlow.

Gradually the case took shape. A tank-transporter incident in 1951 gave fuel for the fire to stoke up the burning ambition of the people to be rid of traffic. Still nothing was done.

But when eventually the two-ton limit was imposed on the white-painted, creaking suspension bridge, the chips were really down. Plans for an entirely new bridge were put forward—as they had been in 1932 when the by-pass plan was first mooted. All sorts of people then became involved. The preservationists were active, vocal and volatile. They were adamant that Marlow Bridge must be preserved. The only way this could be done was to by-pass the town.

While there may have been some people who wanted to see the old bridge go, they kept quiet. The Marlow Bridge Preservation Society was formed. There was a debate on television between the treasurer, F. S. Wedlake, a prominent lawyer in the town as well as

Clerk to the Justices at that time, and the Buckinghamshire County Council engineer, Mr. Frankland.

The local chamber of trade followed the policy laid down by the bridge preservation society, that of keeping and repairing the bridge to a five tons weight restriction and by-passing the town. Marlow Society, an amenity body interested not only in architecture, history, antiquities, but with trying to establish a good all-round environment, also sub-scribed to this view.

The Marlow Society even called in the national press and gave them a guided tour of the 1932 by-pass line. The resulting publicity at national and local level may have influenced authority or not, but within a short time of that press conference, the planners announced they had thought again about the by-pass, and they had decided to expunge the old by-pass route.

For a time there was total disbelief in the town, but then the planners announced they had thought up a new by-pass line, much farther to the east which would mean less noise for the town from the road, and that the new bridge could be sited well downstream and would not overshadow or detract from existing buildings and amenities.

So finally the new line was adopted and in 1970 the first of the machines to prepare the way moved in. In 1972 the new route was opened and after over four and a quarter millions of pounds had been spent, everyone was happy.

But they were all happy only because away back in the early 60s a thorough repair job was done on the old suspension bridge. This was an ingenious piece of work that does credit to everyone involved.

It was finally agreed in 1964 that the suspension bridge would have to be repaired. The workmen arrived and instead of commencing to demolish the bridge, they built a new wooden road surface over the existing decking. It was then that the evils and ravages of war were exposed. Before the second world war the bridge's moving parts were oiled and greased regularly every quarter. This vital work was suspended due to the war and never resumed. Coat after coat of white paint was slapped over the linkages and finally some of these began to seize up and fracture. The suspenders snapping were the first indications to the engineers that something was radically wrong.

They acted quickly. Up went the two tons weight restrictions with massive barriers only high enough to allow through the lightest of vans. A system of traffic lights was installed as the route was only one-way.

Eventually the bridge was re-opened to traffic, once the aerial highway had been dis-mantled. The five tons limit still remained, but the refurbished bridge was a better structure than Tierney Clark could ever have made in his day.

The restored bridge has steel chains and the decking is of metal plates coated in epoxy resin, that might never need to be resurfaced. One thing which went a long way to shorten the life of Tierney Clark's masterpiece, apart from the lack of oiling and greasing, was the additional weight thrown down over the years on the road surface.

When men tried to remove the tarmacadamed surface they were astounded to find that successive layers had built up to a massive 18 inches thickness in places and the estimated total amount of road metal taken off was put at 350 tons. Much of this spoil went to surface Westhorpe Road.

Coincidentally, while the controversy about retaining the bridge in its old form and the provision of a new by-pass raged, there were some harsh things being said about car parking in the town centre.

Marlow, now a small spot of 1,646 acres as an urban district, was still a centre for surrounding villages. Even people from much larger towns not too far distant made regular shopping trips to Marlow because of the freedom of car parking in the main streets—or most of them.

When authority decided to impose restrictions these were opposed tenaciously by the shopkeepers. And the biggest weapon they had in their armoury was the lack of car parks.

At the junction of Dean Street and Spittal Square were two large rough areas that had been the sites of former properties. These were used under sufferance of the Bucks County Council as temporary car parks, but their life was not expected to be great.

The condition of these two areas attracted much fury from traders and road users alike, especially in winter. The Urban Council decided to provide a large central car park at the rear of the Crown Hotel. The Dean Street 'bomb sites' were properly surfaced and to supplement these two facilities as well as a spacious, though by motorists' standards, isolated car park in Pound Lane, more car parks were provided in West Street, Station Approach and Institute Road.

As a result of all these developments, Marlow suddenly became an attractive shopping centre. Still on the planners' books is a scheme to lay a dual-carriageway through the town but leaving the existing shopping centre as a pedestrian precinct.

Lynch-pin in this grandiose plan is to service all shops by deliveries to their rear accesses. Since the Town Centre Report for Marlow was issued in 1962, the plan is within an ace of coming about following recent developments on the south side of Spittal Street in the grounds of New Court.

In 1972, some five years after the steam trains were replaced by diesel-engined carriages, the last locomotive to operate the 'Donkey' service returned to the town. This was to mark the centenary of the opening of the line and it was later estimated that over 50,000 people visited Marlow and Bourne End that day.

The old railway station at Marlow was demolished to aid the laying out of the industrial estate in 1968 and now only an open platform denotes the end of the line.

Several attempts were made over the years to form 'bus companies, with a view to providing truly local services. Most made little impact but in 1925 Marlow and District Motor Services Limited, with headquarters in Glade Road commenced running three services with two 'buses. These services ran to Maidenhead, High Wycombe and Henley. Additional vehicles were bought and at its peak the firm, with a garage in Victoria Road, was travelling an average of 5,500 miles a week, carrying many thousands of people and parcels.

Eventually all 'bus services in the area were taken over by the Thames Valley Traction Company, which in turn was merged with the Aldershot and District Company to become the Alder Valley Company. Latterly the company has linked with the National enterprise.

The 'buses, in their way, went a long way to bring the railway service to death's door. They in turn, were forced into a corner by hire-purchase as the vast majority of people found easy financial facilities of benefit to buy their own forms of personal transport such as motor-scooters, motor cycles and cars. And today commercial traffic on the river is but a memory. Joy seeking pleasure boat-owners and hirers and large steamers have it all their own way.

ABOVE: A typical 19th century sailing barge on the Bisham reach.

CENTRE: The first bridge.

BELOW: The second bridge.

ABOVE LEFT: Third bridge designer, John Tierney Clark.

ABOVE RIGHT: Barges at Rolls Wharf on the Berkshire bank.

BELOW: The third bridge.

ABOVE: The 19th century road to the bridge.

BELOW: Edwardian tranquillity and passenger pleasure-craft.

ABOVE: Vessels had to be hauled through the centre opening in the weir after the first 'flash lock' was introduced.

CENTRE: The 'pound lock' came into use in 1826, with hand-operated sluices and the first lock-keeper's house.

BELOW: Powered sluice gates and a new home for the keeper were introduced in the 1960's.

ABOVE: Waggons hauled heavy goods in the 19th century.

CENTRE: Smart turnout at the Red Lion.

BELOW: Pre-1914 motors replace the Red Lion carriage, and

INSET: Pause for rest in Quarry Woods, when the open cart
was the only way to travel unless you walked.

ABOVE: 'The Marlow Donkey'—later absorbed by the GWR.

BELOW: Steam trains and rail freight diminished, and died in the 1960's, and so did Marlow's old station. Workmen start demolition.

INSET: Engine No 1450, the last locomotive to haul Marlow's trains by steam, returned in 1972. Today it works in the West Country.

ABOVE : People who live in riverside towns get their feet wet. Floods were
frequent in the last century—South Place did not escape.

CENTRE : Brook street, now Station road, was often awash.

BELOW : Even in the late 1960s, the river had its way in
newly built Alder Meadows.

39

ABOVE LEFT: 1962 saw a two-
lights caused queues

BELOW LEFT: Under the ca
in an adv

ABOVE RIGHT: Work was
the makings of

CENTRE RIGHT: After restora
was inevitable, and in 1971 wo
aesthetically in the Marlo

BELOW: December

…raffic using the bridge; traffic
…nine mile diversions.

…d structure was exposed—
…decay.

…rsued round the clock—
…construction.

…affic was outlawed, a by-pass
…d another bridge was built—
…f functional grace.

…ew route opened.

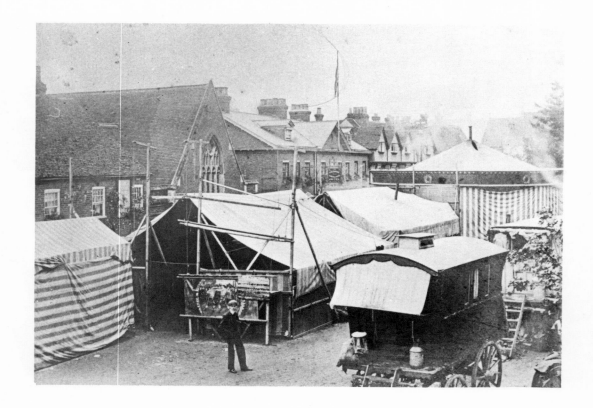

ABOVE: In 1859 Market Place was dominated by the Crown, and the Town Hall, complete with its clocktower and open arches.

BELOW: Tents and carousels clogged the Causeway when Marlow Fair came to town—until 1903.

Markets Fair

In the closing days of the existence of the Marlow Urban Council in 1973-74 a lobby of opinion tried hard to re-establish a market in Marlow. The idea is still alive though it is unlikely that any authority would accede to a request for a market or fair to be held in the streets as was the case before the 20th century.

With trading established in Marlow by 1183, burgage or civic rights (to land) were obtained by then, and by the 13th century the burgesses paid rent of 13 marks and the market was established by 1227/8. The town demanded then that the justices settle a disputed ½d per measure of corn taken by the Earl of Gloucester's bailiffs, against the prevailing customs. In 1260 the Earl purchased the market rights from the Crown—there was already a forum, or market place.

With an abundance of sheep grazing around Marlow, it is not surprising that there was also a wool fair in the mediaeval period.

The earliest reference to a fair was Edward II's grant in 1324 to Hugh Spencer at his manor of Chipping Marlow. Langley in 1797 recorded that 'there are two (fairs) held in the year: one on the 2nd of May, now only for toys and trifling commodities; and the other on the 29th of October, for horses, cattle, cheese and other articles'. He added: 'The shew of horses, chiefly for agricultural uses, has been very considerable of late years'.

Then turning from fairs to markets, Langley observed: 'The market is held on Saturdays, but is ill supplied; and the little corn trade here is chiefly carried on by sample'.

The Second Town or Market Hall later to become the Crown Inn, was built as a result of political ambition. Thomas Williams, having completed Temple House and anxious to secure the family interest with his electors, employed Samuel Wyatt to design and Benjamin Gray to build a new market house. This replaced the old timber building, described by Langley as 'a very miserable heavy building of timber', and 'a disgrace to the town'. The new one was completed at Owen Williams' behest, for Thomas died before his ambition was fulfilled. When built, its arches were open, and it was described by Sheahan in 1861 as 'a substantial edifice'.

In 1599 John Rotherham of Seymours had left £40 towards procuring a charter of incorporation and reviving a market to be kept weekly, the profits of which were to be vested in the corporation. In 1813 Lyson wrote: 'but his intention never took effect. The market which appears to have been then discontinued, has been revived and is held on Saturdays'.

By 1888 the meat market was held in the Town Hall basement and the fairs, originally one a year, increased to two by the 14th century, extending to several days until they eventually became shorter and shorter, and finally died out.

The October cattle market went out of existence almost at the same time of the start of the second world war in 1939. Until then the cattle market had been held in an area bounded by Station Approach and Lock Road on which now stands the Royal British Legion headquarters and a car park.

Here the land was marked off with pens and barriers. Until the early 1960s, there was still a railway line running up to buffers and a wharf in the triangle of land between Station Approach and Station Road.

Cattle trucks were shunted up to this wharf on market days and the cattle driven across Station Approach to the market. Now local farmers have to go farther afield to buy and sell their stock, to such places as High Wycombe, Reading, and Thame.

Marlow Fair, more an entertainment than a commercial event by then, died out a lot earlier. It was in 1900 that Marlow Urban Council began to think seriously of ridding the main streets of the booths, stalls and caravans that descended on Marlow annually.

The one man the council had to consult was General Owen Williams of Temple House for it was he who was entitled to collect the fair tolls. His immediate reaction was to ask if the council had any indication of the wishes of the local people.

Presumably the council had not done so as their minutes show they started to canvass the town, and eventually the citizens, by 'a large majority', voted in favour of abolition. In 1903 the council successfully applied to the Local Government Board for an Order abolishing the street fair.

After that it was held for a time in Star Meadow, an area off Wycombe Road which was later to become the temporary home of Marlow Football Club before they moved to their present ground 'over the hedge'. But a lot of the character and atmosphere went, and the fair steadily slipped into decline. The one person who gained out of the decision was General Williams, for it was agreed to compensate him for the loss of his fair tolls in the sum of £200.

The fairmen's 'vardo's' lined the High street, and
the local police force watched points.

44

Masters of Trade

It used to be said at one time in Marlow there were just two industries in the town . . . the making of beer and the drinking of it! While this was an over-simplification it would have been easy to understand in the late 19th and early 20th centuries.

But commerce in Marlow goes back a good deal further in time. Trade in the 13th century was dominated by wheat, hides and cloth, though the mills of Marlow were established by 1086—one at Little Marlow, and one at Great Marlow.

Fisheries yielded prolifically as well in Norman times—the two Marlows produced 1500 eels between them annually, and Medmenham a further 1000.

The river provided other revenue; custody of the swans gave rise to numerous grants in the 15th century, and by 1554 Lord Paget secured the rights to a 'swanne marke' and to the swans themselves. A game of swans on the Thames and the marks belonging to it were left by John Sandes of Great Marlow to his son Henry in 1555. By the nineteenth century, ownership was vested in the Crown and in the Dyers' and Vintners' Companies, who send swanhoppers to count and mark the birds each year. As Royal property, they cannot be caught or killed by sportsmen.

Mills loomed large in Marlow's 19th century commercial life. The paper mills of William Wright & Sons vied with Wethered's brewery for local labour. In the 18th century, Thomas Williams manufactured brass and copper products at Temple mills. Lace was a major local cottage industry—mainly made at Borlase School—and local craftsmen turned pottery at both Marlow and Medmenham, their product once gracing the frieze of the Law Society's hall in Chancery Lane. There was a chair factory, and in addition to lace, baby linen, satin stitch work and embroidery kept workers' hands occupied. Thimbles were another local product and corn milling continued.

Brewing was evidently a Marlovian industry in 1690 when James Fish was indicted for retailing a cask of ale and a cask of 'the best hop-brewed beer' to William Hopkins, an unlicensed alehouse keeper. Every year saw accusations in court of the unlicensed sale of beer and the keeping of unlicensed or disorderly alehouses.

In 1706 the brewing industry was well established, for a barge, the Little Dove, sank opposite Harleyford House, containing quantities of malt and in 1711 another barge, The Angell, also sank near the town.

But dominating the industrial scene in Victorian times was The Brewery. It belonged to the Wethered family and they were quite easily the largest employers of labour.

Although Thomas Wethered and Sons Limited has now been merged into the Whitbread group, work continues in the brewery, just off the High Street, and there is a wide catchment area of public houses, hotels and clubs serviced by the brown drays, carrying locally brewed beer.

Origins of the firm are a little obscure, though historians put its establishment in 1758. It is interesting also to note from the 19th century records that they described the enterprise as 'the chief Brewery in Marlow', which confirms that there were others engaged in the beer business too.

It is accepted by the firm that a member of the Wethered family was in business in 1758, although Thomas Wethered had not yet been born. His father, George, lived in Marlow. In 1744 he had married Elizabeth Gibbons, daughter of a brewer in St Peter Street. This may be the reason behind it all, as it is likely George acquired an interest in brewing from his father-in-law. After the death of Elizabeth in 1757 George married his second wife, Anne Reynolds.

In his Will of 1783 George described himself as a Brewer. He confirmed the gift to his son George (by his first wife) of the remainder of a Lease from the late Henry Smith of a dwellinghouse, malthouse and appurtenances being on the east side of the High Street in Great Marlow. The Brewery today is on the west side.

The house and malthouse were then in the occupation of his son George, who was also to receive under the Will the stock, utensils and implements.

To his son Thomas (by his second wife Anne) he bequeathed 'the Lease of the malt-house, maltkiln, yard, earthouse and appurtenances situated and being in the High Street of Great Marlow on the west side and which I hold of William Clayton, Esq, and also all my stock of malt, barley, utensils and implements belonging to the said malthouse and business carried on and also all my stock and utensils in the Brewing business'.

There are no plans attached to the title deeds of the present Brewery that stands between High Street and Portlands Alley, flanked by Pound Lane, though it does seem clear it was not occupied by a Wethered until Thomas Wethered leased it in 1788 from William Clayton for 99 years at £18 per annum. The premises are referred to in the title deeds as 'formerly Miss Freeman's Boarding School and the Three Tuns Tavern'.

Nor is there any mention of a brewery as such until Thomas purchased the Freehold in 1796 for £400 'with the new brewhouse, stable, storehouses and premises lately erected and built'.

From all this it can be surmised that George Wethered (1714-1783) was a brewer in Marlow. His eldest son George (1745-1820) lived in a house and a malthouse on the east side of High Street. These premises were demolished in the mid-1960s when they became unsafe. On the site now stand three shops with flats above.

His other son Thomas (1761-1849), worked in a brewery somewhere on the west side of High Street, though definitely not the site of the present brewery.

No information exists as to what became of the younger George. It was his father's wish though: 'That my said sons do deal with each other in their several businesses as I am fully persuaded it will be to their mutual advantage'.

Piers D. Power in 1959 wrote of the disappearing younger George: 'It is surmised that Thomas's business prospered and perhaps outgrew the premises his father had left him, or the Lease expired, for there is no doubt that Thomas leased the present brewery premises in 1788 and in 1796 bought the Freehold of the property—which then included the new brewhouse . . . etc'. This is confirmed by a stone engraved 'T.W. 1788' which is outside the back door of the offices and in 1819 there was a memorandum stating: 'A brewhouse and other buildings have, since the purchase of the estate, been built on the premises by Thomas Wethered'.

Several other stones bearing dates indicate the progress made on the brewery site. In

1791 The White House on the north side of the brewery was leased to Thomas and in 1820 he purchased the Freehold.

It seems probable that although George may have had a small brewery on the west side of High Street in 1758, it was not until after his death in 1783 that his son Thomas, in 1788, really founded the firm of Thomas Wethered and Sons on the site where the Brewery still stands to this day.

Thomas Wethered's sons, Owen and Lawrence William, became partners in the business and Thomas retired in 1845, living at Remnantz, in West Street. He purchased this in 1813 after it ceased to be the Royal Military College. He died in 1849.

Owen died in 1862 and his sons Thomas Owen Wethered of Seymour Court and Owen Peel Wethered of The White House became partners and were joined by their brother Robert Peel Wethered in 1870, though he died three years later.

In 1890 Owen Peel's sons, Francis and Walter, became partners and on the retirement of Thomas Owen in the same year his son-in-law, John Danvers Power, joined them. This arrangement continued until 1899 when the business was turned into a Limited Liability Company with Owen Peel as chairman.

Mechanisation had been introduced in part during the Victorian era and once into the 20th century the company quickly saw the advantages of machines. The bottlery was opened in 1901 and in 1903 a chimney sprouted. This was all part of the electric lighting plant installed by the company engineer, V. B. Butt.

Mechanical transport, too, started to replace the resplendent horse-drawn brewers' drays that covered thousands of miles annually on their distribution rounds. The first lorries were steam-driven and they came on the scene around 1905. They comprised trailers behind traction engines, and though Marlow Bridge presented some difficulties because of the weight restrictions imposed even in those days, the men got round it by an ingenious method.

The trailer was horse-drawn over the bridge after the engine had first crossed over! Later when draymen were returning to the brewery from the Berkshire side they made use of a telephone direct line to the brewery. The phone was sited at the bottom of Bisham Hill and a crew would turn out from the brewery to tow the lorries across. The petrol-engined drays appeared around 1911.

Colonel F. E. Stevens became managing-director in 1908 on the death of Colonel Owen Peel Wethered. His son, Lieutenant Colonel Francis Owen Wethered, succeeded at the head of the Board Room table.

In 1914 Wethered's ale received national recognition when, at the Brewers' Exhibition, they were awarded the Championship Gold Medal. J. D. Power left the Board in 1916 and the following year Walter Wethered died. J. L. Holland, head brewer, was made a director. On the death of Lieutenant Colonel F. O. Wethered in 1922, Piers Danvers Power who joined the Board the previous year, was joined by John D. Power who became chairman.

Sir Richard Garton and Charles Garton bought a large number of Ordinary Shares in 1926 and the latter joined the Board. The following year Lieutenant Colonel Joseph R. Wethered, a great grandson of the founder, who had succeeded Colonel Stevens as first general manager then later as managing-director, was elected chairman of the Board on the death of John Danvers Power. Also in 1927, Williams' Royal Stag Brewery at Wooburn was purchased. This firm had 35 licensed houses.

In 1942, Lt Col J. R. Wethered died. Stanley Garton of Danesfield, Medmenham, became managing-director with his cousin, K. G. Durrant as part-time assistant. Piers D.

Power was elected chairman. Francis John Wethered, son of Lt Col F. O. Wethered by his second wife, joined the board in the same year but before a year was up he lost his life at sea when the ship in which he was travelling was torpedoed.

Commander O. F. M. Wethered, RN, was elected to the Board in 1945 and three years later on the death of Mr Stanley Garton, Piers D. Power was appointed managing-director as well as chairman. Messrs Strong and Company of Romsey, Limited, bought the shares of Thomas Wethered and Sons Limited and the Board was reconstituted. In 1950 Strange's Aldermaston Brewery was purchased and three years later S. H. Higgs, Limited, Lion Brewery at Reading was bought. The firm was finally taken over by Whitbread's.

In addition to providing employment for a large number of local people, Wethereds have been the means of providing the majority of the community's leisure facilities, having by far the largest share of the control of local public houses and hotels. In the 18th century they sprang up like mushrooms, in the form of alehouses and beer-houses, not least in Dean Street.

Dean Street must have been quite a place. By present day standards the area was a slum. The houses, small, cramped, terraced affairs housed hundreds of people. Marlow folk still recall how the police would only go up Dean Street in pairs and with truncheons drawn!

The local wags called the tumbledown area The City. And why not? At the Lane End of Dean Street was The Bank of England; at the Common Slough end (that was what Spittal Square was called in those days) was The Mint; and between the two stood The Royal Exchange.

These bearers of famous names were but the tip of the iceberg. Take a look at the list of beerhouses that had licences renewed by the court of 1874: The Fighting Cocks; The Anchor; The Travellers Friend; The Fox and Pheasant; Alma; The Crown and Cushion; The Cherry Tree; The Nag's Head; The Verney Arms in addition to the trio of houses that made up The City. There was also an alehouse in Dean Street, The Jolly Maltsters.

In those days the Licensing Area included the parish of Ackhampstead (a detached piece of Oxfordshire in the area bounded by Frieth, Lane End and Chisbeach, known today as Chisbridge). There was a beerhouse called The Black Boy there. Today's houses were there then, but quite a number of others have since gone: The Plough at Fawley; The Royal Oak, Frieth; The Jolly Cricketers, Bovingdon Green; The Scalemakers' Arms, Well End and The Dashwood Arms, Flackwell Heath.

Gone, too, are a number of alehouses. The Greyhound in Spittal Street; The Three Tuns, West Street; The Horns, Chapel Street; The Black Boy in Church Passage and The Barge Pole in St Peter Street.

In 1723 there were four mills in Great Marlow, belonging to John and Mary Ferrers and by 1797 there were corn and paper mills on the riverside. These survived in business well into the present century, several pieces of machinery dating to 1874, 1876 and 1882. In May 1939 the mills and the site were offered for sale at £2,000 freehold. They were eventually sold and during the second world war were used for storage purposes. The building was demolished in 1965 and a flat development replaced it.

Behind the Two Brewers public house in St Peter Street there used to be a furniture factory in a large barn, now part of The Minnows. Women and children earned sixpence for caning chair seats. The factory closed just before the 1914 war.

Cottage industries abounded in the town for centuries. Lace making was a great source of revenue to the women of the town while men would comb the hedgerows and commons and woods seeking out the best type of wood to make skewers. Farming had always played a major part in local life, and much of the labour force was recruited in Marlow.

Some women engaged in 'stone picking' at the turn of the century. This was a laborious chore requiring much patience as flints had to be first gathered from the fields, then graded. They were used in the construction of 'waterbound roads', the flints being covered with water and soil, then steam-rollered. For 'a load' of flints the reward was the princely sum of one shilling.

Secluded, the town was an ideal place for the shadow-factory plan dreamed up during World War II by Lord Beaverbrook, Minister for Aircraft Production.

Marlow Place, former annex of the Royal Military College when in Marlow and residence of George II while Prince of Wales, was ideal for just such a 'shadow factory'. Vital small components for aircraft were manufactured in considerable quantities. It was discovered when the cellars were inspected by security men that a tunnel sloped downwards in the direction of the river. For years there had been legends about a passage under the Thames to Bisham Abbey, but the security men were not in antiquarian mood. Just in case saboteurs knew of the other end of the tunnel they bricked it up!

This brief soujourn into the field of aviation was to be the forerunner of another in post-war years. A company started in the kitchen of his Chelsea home set Geoffrey Charles on the road to success. A former officer in the wartime RAF, he developed a static discharger for aircraft, then set about making them in Marlow.

There was another legacy from the war. As bombs crashed down on London in the 'blitz', Greenwich Sawmills decided to evacuate. They chose Marlow and established a vast yard behind Dedmere Road as it was in close proximity to the railhead.

At the end of the war the company continued actively in business and it was they who created the precedent for the area to be further industrialised. Over the past 25 years the area first colonised by the sawmills has grown and expanded to include numerous firms whose products are household words.

LEFT: Heir to the Domesday milling heritage—this one time paper-mill became a warehouse after World War II.

RIGHT: John Turk, the Queen's Swanmaster.

ABOVE: Marlow's mill stood proudly until the 1960's.

BELOW: Then it fell victim to demolition.

50

ABOVE: Homes replaced Marlow's mill—designed in a genuine attempt to maintain the flavour of the original structure.

CENTRE: These local skewers were once a staple cottage industry.

BELOW: Eels provided income—for a thousand years. Traps were set by the bridge and the weir.

LEFT: For centuries, farming was the main local source of income, and Marlow's farmworkers dressed like this.

RIGHT: A medieaval farmworker's billhook, left in the Thames at Marlow.

BELOW: A Marlow bargee's bootscoop. (Bucks County Museum).

53

ABOVE LEFT: George Wethered (1714-1783), founder of the Marlow Brewery. (Whitbread & Co Ltd).

ABOVE RIGHT: 1920s medals won by brewery drivers.

BELOW: The award winning draymen.

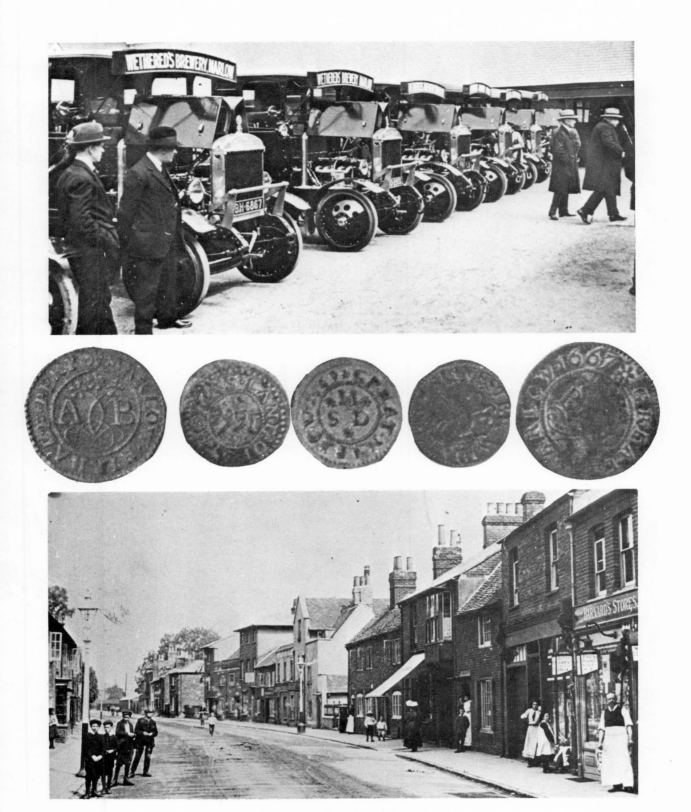

ABOVE: An array of drays.

CENTRE: Trade tokens struck by local traders in the
small change famine 1666-1669. (Bucks County Museum).

BELOW: Chapel street, *c* 1912.

55

ABOVE LEFT: 19
sported tall ha

ABOVE CENTRE: As
corn, tea and provi

ABOVE RIGHT: Spit
in the

BELOW LEFT

BELOW RIGHT: Th
highly recommended with

...gh street tradesmen
...ocked windows.

...urned A. Ilsley dealt in
...ivered to your door.

...a commercial flavour
...entury.

...street in 1902.

...Hotel, Spittal street—
... at the turn of the century.

ABOVE: The Crown had absorbed the old Town Hall by the 1890s.

BELOW: Transfer complete, the Crown stayed in the Town Hall,
but shops and flats in the old Crown were empty by the 1970s.

ABOVE: The bridge end of High street, 1909.

BELOW: Development has changed the skyline 64 years later.

59

ABOVE: West street, early 1900s.

BELOW: West street and Market Square, 1903.

60

ABOVE: In 1968 changes were few in West street, though the obelisk lamp had turned from gas to electricity, and some windows had disappeared.

BELOW: Station road remains much as it was here, in 1921.

61

newman & Chalk,

HIGH STREET, MARLOW.

◆ ◆ ◆ ◆ ◆ ◆ ◆

IRONMONGERS. . .

. FISHING TACKLE.

. . ILLUMINATIONS.

ABOVE LEFT: Morgan's of High street, near the Square,
gave credit, despite advertising cash terms.

ABOVE RIGHT: Times may change, but one shop still displays
its wares as fearlessly today as in 1902.

BELOW: The Compleat Angler in more modest early post-war guise.

First gravel pits, then contention over a silo: now an industrial
estate fills the one-time timber yard. (Aerofilms Ltd).

ABOVE: Great Marlow Church, with passing river trade,
in the 19th century.

BELOW LEFT AND RIGHT: Two Marlow Parish priests of 1430-40
once lived on in brass relief in the church.

CENTRE BELOW: John Warner was Rector of Marlow in 1421—
he too was once immortalised in brass in his own church.

In Praise of God

If the Saxons worshipped at Marlow, there is no trace or record of their church. The first known parish church dated back to the early 12th century, and sometime in the next century a priory was established at Little Marlow (Minchin Marlow), as well as Little Marlow's parish church. The following century Medmenham church was built, though Medmenham Abbey was founded in 1200. The Normans appear to have been the first to establish Christianity on a broad base in the Marlow area.

There have been three Churches on or near to the present site of All Saints' Parish Church. The first was built of the local 'clunch' stone—or hard chalk. It was subject to flooding. The foundations were affected and the tower and part of the spire were rebuilt in 1745.

In 1773 the first pound-lock was constructed on the River Thames and this had the effect of raising the river level permanently. The Churchwardens are recorded as paying in 1777 to Richard Darby 'Six guineas for the large cast-iron Brazier wherein to make a large Charcoal Fire to warm the Church'. This information is supplemented with an addition: 'NB It has been found very comfortable'.

But if the brazier made the inside of the Church acceptable, outside the river had other ideas. The entire Church was completely surrounded by flood water on December 30, 1821. The water rose so rapidly that the congregation inside were cut off and ladies had to be carried by men to dry land.

One lady, renowned for her meanness, was told as she reached the centre of the inundated forecourt, carried by a local fellow, that unless she produced her shilling forthwith she would be dropped in the deepest part!

Part of the Church collapsed in 1830. James Savage, well known in the architectural world at that time, reported: 'The Church is occasionally inundated with water leaving a durable mark on the pew framing 17 inches above the paving. The mischievous consequences of such a state to the health of parties attending worship, and as well to the Fabric, which is covered with green vegetation, are such as call loudly for an amendment'.

Charles Inwood was employed in 1832 to build an entirely new Church. In old engravings of this second building, the Church looks a squat little rectangle in white brick with a small tower and spire. It was built on 'higher and healthier ground'—the lessons of the floods having obviously been learned.

Forty years later a chancel was added. Later still J. Olrid Scott inserted arcades in the nave, removed the galleries, remodelled the tower, changed the windows and raised the flat roof to a pitched one.

By this time the Parish Church began to look much as we know it today. Considerable trouble was taken to maintain memorials and monuments from the former Church and now there are well over 150, especially as in the past eight years pews have begun to appear to replace the chairs that were used by congregations. Each pew is a memorial to someone.

The Parish Registers and the Churchwardens' accounts date back to 1592. The first incumbent was William de Neketon (1204) who was replaced in 1244 by William de Staneway. King John was the Patron on a vacancy of Tewkesbury Abbey. The first Vicar was William Warda in 1495.

Midway through the 19th century the Church had such large congregations that it was decided to build a second Church in the northern part of Marlow. Holy Trinity Church was consecrated in 1852. It closed in 1975 due to economics.

One old building, hard by Marlow bridge, had religious connections. The conventual barn of Bisham Abbey, variously used as a coal depot and a POW prison, was pulled down in 1878 and the timber went towards the new Lane End church.

Marlow vicarage was once on the west of the High Street, moved to the east side, and was subsequently replaced by a building on the site of the Swan PH in 1863. The parsonage house behind the church in St Peter's Street originated in the 14th century, was rebuilt in the 17th century and subsequently enlarged, but still included the original hall. Part of it was known as the Deanery, due to a confusion between the name of a one time owner (Dean) and the modern RC convent nearby.

Marlow had, apart from the church, three chapels within the parish. A chantry chapel was attached to the church, another was associated with a hermitage, and gave names to Chapel Street and Chapel End, and the old manor of Harleyford also boasted its own chapel, pulled down in 1775.

Widmer Manor, once a hamlet of 100 people, was held first by the Knights Hospitallers, and then by the Knights Templars until their dissolution in 1307. The Hospitallers built a chapel and The Templars held their chapters secretly in the crypt beneath. Centuries later the chapel was in use as a brewhouse.

The Benedictine nunnery of Minchin Marlow was not a significant house. No great family supported it, though Leland states that Geoffrey Lord Spencer was the founder, probably wrongly.

Certainly by the time of King John, the nunnery existed, and it may well have been founded in the reign of Henry II. In 1230 Agnes de Anvers, or Danvers was patroness, and Matilda de Anvers was prioress.

The Priory was suppressed on June 23, 1536, the prioress then being Margaret Vernon. The Commissioners reported that it was worth £23 3s 7d in rents. At that time there were two nuns with two servants and two women servants as well as a priest. The bells and lead were worth £5 10s 8d, and the building was in good condition. There were no debts and the goods were worth £17 0s. 2d. The priory owned 8 acres of woodland. Before the commissioners acted, there had been six nuns.

Margaret Vernon wrote to Thomas Cromwell, offering her resignation, for which she received an appointment as Abbess of Malling, Kent—which was dissolved shortly after. She then received a £40 pension. Her letter is loyal and long suffering: '. . . not a lyttyll to my dyscomforte, nevertheless I must be content with the Kynges plesure . . .' and later 'Trustynge and nothynge dowptynge In yowre goodness that ye wyll so provyd for vs that we shall have syche onest lyvynge that we shall be not dreven be necessyte nether to begge nor to fall to no other vnconvenyence . . .'

Commissioner William Cavendish must have been impressed with Prioress Margaret, for he wrote also to Cromwell on her behalf: 'I shall therfore most humblie bysiche yor maistershipp . . . to be good unto her . . .'

The priory's possessions went to Bisham Abbey, itself fated to dissolution two years later.

The priory itself survived for over a century—a tower, hall, chapter, chapel house, dormitory, and farm buildings. The conventual hall was demolished in 1740. A farmhouse was built from the materials—probably Abbey Farm.

Hugh de Bolebec's grandson founded Medmenham or Mednam Abbey. In 1086 Medmenham was known as Medemeha and Bolebec held the manor; Hugh the younger founded the Cistercian Abbey of Woburn, and his brother Walter bestowed on that estate the Manor of Mednam. The Abbey was founded as a cell of the parent foundation in 1200. Originally Woburn monks stayed briefly at the new abbey. By 1212 Cistercian monks had settled there, and by 1256 Roger was the first abbot. The last, in 1536, was John Talbot.

After the dissolution, the manor and the abbey site were granted to Thomas and Robert Moore. The buildings gradually fell into disrepair. Only the remains of the old conventual chapel remained when Sir Francis Dashwood restored the buildings in the 18th century. Here he founded the Knights of St Francis of Wycombe, wrongly called the Monks of Medmenham, and often confused with the Hellfire Club started by Philip, Duke of Wharton.

Twenty-four men of rank were admitted and celebrated perversions of religious ceremonies as well as discussing politics. Among them was Frederick, Prince of Wales, and they were in Opposition to the government of the day. By 1762 they had fallen into disrepute and a satire by John Wilkes brought about the final closure of the 'order' in 1763. Legends proliferated in subsequent years, but the Abbey was eventually again restored in 1898. It became a hotel.

In 1548 the estate itself had been conveyed by the Moores to the Duffield family. In 1778 the Duffield family sold the estate to John Morton, Chief Justice of Chester who resided at Danesfield and from whose widow it was purchased in 1780 by Robert Scott of Crailing, Roxburghshire.

Mr Scott died in 1808 and he left his estates in the neighbouring parish of Hambleden to Charles Scott Murray, his nephew, who was the grandson of John Murray of Philiphaugh, Selkirkshire. He died in 1837 and was succeeded by his son Charles Robert Scott Murray.

Marlow's Roman Catholic Church owes its existence to Charles Robert Scott Murray who was born at the Manor House, Hambleden, on December 28, 1818. In 1841 he became a Conservative Member of Parliament for Buckinghamshire.

While at Eton and Oxford, he developed an interest in the Tractarian movement and in Italy in 1844 was received into the Catholic Church.

On his return to England, Scott Murray resigned his seat in Parliament and soon after married the Hon Amelia Charlotte Lovat Fraser, the daughter of the 14th Lord Lovat, and brought his 20-years-old bride to Danesfield.

Now aged 25, Scott Murray took possession of Oxford Cottage, in Oxford Road, installed Father Peter Coop as priest in charge of the new mission and at the same time engaged Augustus Welby Pugin to draw up plans for a parish church in Marlow as well as a private chapel at Danesfield.

A farmyard was bought in Duck Lane but without revealing the purpose to which the site was to be put. Father W. J. Gaffney, who wrote a short history of the Church in 1974 before his retirement, commented: 'The wisdom of this caution became apparent when it became known that a Catholic Church was to be built and the local outcry expressed the antipathy in the area'.

The foundation stone was laid in July 1845 by Bishop Wareing, Bishop of Areopolis and then Vicar Apostolic of the Eastern District. He was to become Bishop of Northampton five years later when the Catholic hierarchy was restored in this country. The builder of the Church was George Myers of Hull who was responsible for most of Pugin's churches.

It was on July 29, 1846 that Bishop Wareing returned for the Solemn Consecration and sealed in the High Altar, relics of Saint Felix and Saint Constantia. The Lady Altar was also consecrated and relics of the same Saints sealed therein.

Another relic which has caused great interest is a mummified hand. The hand is said to be that of St James the Apostle and had been kept at Reading Abbey until the Dissolution of the Monasteries in the 16th century. It was finally purchased by Mr Scott Murray in 1856 for his private chapel at Danesfield and was finally brought to the St Peter's Church when the estate at Danesfield was sold.

With the dramatic increase in the population of Marlow in the late 1940s and 1950s, it became apparent to the Roman Catholic community in the town that something would have to be done about increasing the accommodation in the Pugin Church. When the Church was consecrated an eyewitness wrote that "the first two rows" were barely filled'.

By 1968 there were 650 people regularly attending Sunday Mass. Clearly there was a desire to retain the original Church and eventually it was decided to make an extension to accommodate an additional 350 people. The work was duly started in 1968 and in 1970 the Bishop of Northampton dedicated the extension.

Early protest against the established church, while rife elsewhere in the county seems restricted to isolated instances in Marlow—though there was a famous occasion when the Salvation Army band was jailed, but this had little to do with religious persuasion. They had simply refused to pay the necessary fee to enable them to play for an open-air service in Market Square.

Nonetheless, when the Bishop visited Great Marlow in 1662, he did find a number of dissidents, including anabaptists, and he also found that some of the congregation had failed to baptise their children. Neither the local lecturer nor the physician were licensed. At Little Marlow the church was 'out of repair' and there was trouble at Medmenham: 'There is not a coverging for the font, nor a flaggon belonging to the communion table, nor the booke of homilies, nor of canons and constitucions ecclesiasticall nor a printed table (of) degrees wherein marriage is prohibited, nor a booke of paper to register the names of strangers that preach, nor a hearsecloth; no surplice.'

Even earlier, the Christian Knights of Widmer may have feared religious persecution, for there is said to have been an underground passage from their chapel to Seymours, though there is no proof.

In the last years of Charles II's reign, when plots were afoot to bring back Catholicism, numerous cases are recorded of 'Popish recusants' in Marlow brought to court. On October 7, 1680 at Chesham, John Brinckhurst of Marlow was presented—'a popish Recusant yett is a Beddrid man with the gowt.'

In 1726, Richard Webb obtained a contract to build a new dissenting chapel in the town, and the Marlow United Reform Church, formerly the Congregational Church built in 1840, restored 1863 and again in 1890 stands on the site of an earlier, 1603 building.

Marlow Baptist Church was built in 1885 in Glade Road, and Marlow Methodist Church went up in 1901 for £2,200 in Spittal Street—so named after the Hospital of St Thomas, mentioned in 1384 as in need of income, and granted property yielding incomes of 100s pa.

The Marlow Corps of the Salvation Army has its headquarters in Crown Road. The Citadel was completed in 1931. Wittington Eventide Homes at Danesfield is also operated by the Salvation Army.

LEFT: All Saints' spire has long dominated the river scene, but its companions have come and gone. Between church and bridge stood the conventual barn of Bisham Abbey.

ABOVE: The Victoria Boathouse replaced the barn.

Still perfectly preserved—the Widmere chapel of the Knights Templars.

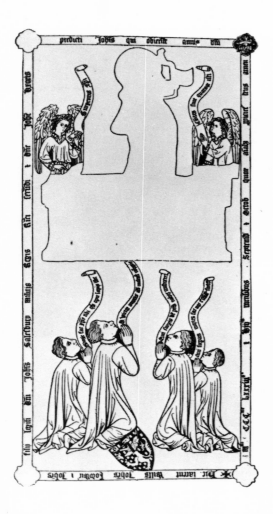

ABOVE: Now flats occupy the conventual barn site.

BELOW LEFT: William, John, Louis and John, sons of Sir John and
Dame Joan Salesbury, 1383/88—once part of All Saints' decor.

BELOW RIGHT: The seal of John of Medmenham, Abbot of
Chertsey, who lived his early life at Medmenham Abbey.

ABOVE: The Old Parsonage in St Peter street—possibly Bucks'
finest example of 14th century domestic architecture.

CENTRE: Medmenham Abbey—Dashwood's clubhouse, Disraeli's home-
from-home (as the Ferry Boat Hotel), and in 1913 restored to domestic use.

BELOW: Danesfield House, near the Abbey—the third building
on the site.

71

LITTLE MARLOW

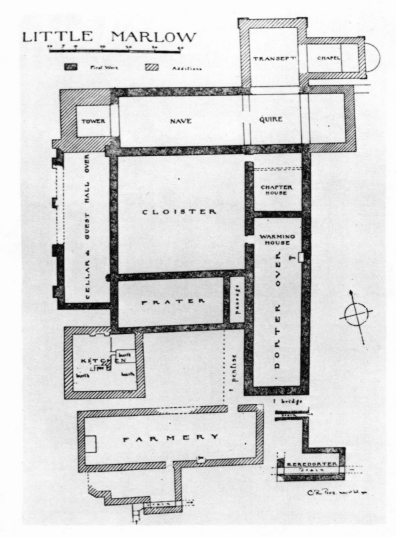

72

CENTRE LEF

CENTRE R

BORDE

e Marlow Priory.
Marlow church.
the Priory.

73

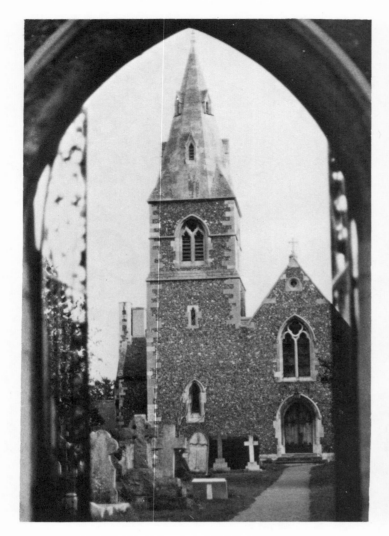

ABOVE LEFT: Pugin's St Peter's RC Church.

ABOVE RIGHT: A Celtic cross marks the resting place of James L. Molloy in St Peter's churchyard. He composed 'Love's Old Sweet Song.'

BELOW: The hand of St James, acquired from Reading Abbey by St Peter's benefactor, Scott Murray.

74

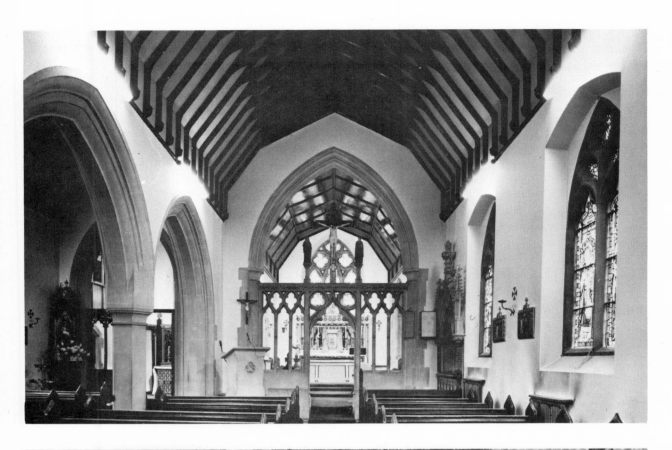

ABOVE: Inside the original RC church.

BELOW: Inside the extension, at the 1971 dedication.

ABOVE: United Reform Church, Quoiting Square—
previously the Congregational Church.

BELOW: The Salvation Army Citadel in Crown road.

76

ABOVE : Consecrated 1852 due to overcrowding at All Saints',
Holy Trinity Church was closed in 1975.

BELOW LEFT : Marlow Methodist Church.

BELOW RIGHT : Marlow Baptist Church, Glade road.

ABOVE : Marlow Bottom, *c* 1929. The tower marks the
isolation hospital.

CENTRE : Forty-five years later.

BELOW : Community spirit in Marlow Bottom—parish
councillors and local children solve the litter problem.

78

The Valley

Apart from Little Marlow and Medmenham, Marlow has a third close neighbour. Marlow Bottom is something of a 20th century enigma. Like Topsy, Marlow Bottom 'just growed'. Practically all the mushroom-like development has taken place in the last 30 years. Before the second world war the valley known as Marlow Bottom was for the most part scrubland, open fields and shacks.

These buildings were thrown up as week-end holiday homes by people from the cities and towns. They had a lot of fun constructing their shacks, and equally enjoyed the facilities once they had completed the work. In most cases the method of construction was simple. Four tall posts at each corner of the intended structure were then interconnected by chicken wire. With one man inside the square and another on the outside they floated cement up the wire to make the walls. When the walls set they simply took a saw and cut out spaces for the doors and window frames which were then put in on another week-end. The roof could be anything from corrugated iron sheeting to close-fitting matchboard, later covered with roofing felt.

But that was before the war. At the end of hostilities people started looking around for somewhere to live. There was never any evidence of a vast design or plan for 'The Valley' as Marlow Bottom is still referred to by its residents. Houses were just built on plots when planning permission was obtained. Gradually the image of the little country lane began to disappear as the bricks and mortar started to flow along the floor of the valley and up the escarpments.

As the houses grew in number and the old shacks and shanties disappeared Marlow Bottom began to take on a character. The people knew what they wanted and were not afraid to say so.

A hard core of pre-war residents, while showing little resentment towards the newcomers living alongside them, took a firm stand when the newcomers began to call for street lights. Said the older folks: 'You knew you were coming to the country and we don't want the town'.

But eventually the street lights did go up. In the wake of the houses have come shops, a club, a public house, numerous factories and industrial enterprises and the village hall, that has satisfied community needs over many years and is now becoming a target for replacement by a community centre.

But it is not all bricks and mortar at Marlow Bottom. The Great Marlow Parish Council steered the purchase of a large area of land adjacent to the new school and secured it as a playing field, which is in course of being laid out.

A satellite church of All Saints' Parish Church in Marlow was dedicated on May 9, 1965. The Church of St Mary the Virgin is a dual-purpose building used as a hall for social functions as well as a place of worship.

19th century Marlow, when the Borough boundaries were the
subject of discussion and change. (Marlow Library).

80

A Town of Consequence

Marlow and its neighbouring manors were first to experience a rudimentary form of administration under the Saxons, when the original manorial holdings were defined. With the coming of the Normans, local government, based on the same, or similar property considerations became more sophisticated, but still the landowners took the local decisions, albeit by permission of the Crown.

With the 1183 granting of burgage rights, the town itself began to feel its way towards some independence, but it was the river bridge that first gave Marlovians some economic rights, and with them a modest degree of power. Even so, the mesne borough was still held by the Lord of Great Marlow manor. He and his successors variously obtained privileges such as the return of writs, regalian rights, view of frankpledge, common fine, courts leet and baron, and free warren. Effectively these meant the lord held the courts and dispensed justice; complaints between townsfolk came to him for settlement, and he could hunt where he willed. But he also had obligations, including the provision of a pillory and tumbril. Such rights lasted into the 18th century.

The borough organisation, such as it was, was slim in the 13th century, when the townsfolk were associated through the chantry of St Mary. By 1394 they had some control over the bridge—the lifeline to the town.

Warden de Waltinton received an oak in 1227 for bridge works, and there were frequent grants for pontage—charges to users to go towards bridge upkeep. In 1310 the bridge was decayed and partially broken, so clearly the allowance was insufficient, but when the Despensers fell from grace, the burgesses seized the opportunity to strengthen their hand, and acquired more grants. In 1565 landowners were making a contribution—John Seymour who came from a burghal family, made his will. He left an oak a year for sixty years for repairs, with the proviso that the bridgemasters paid for felling and carriage.

The chantry was first recorded in 1387, when burgesses were presented, and in 1394 it was set down that their rights had existed 'from time immemorial'. But in 1547 the chantry was dissolved along with all others—a victim of the religious turmoil of Henry VIII's break with Rome.

During its life the chantry moved tentatively towards some form of care for the needy and some form of education for the town's children. Priest Sir James Gray was paid £6 13s 4d salary and 'allowed to teach children and to help to minister in the quier.' Again, 13s was paid to 'two poor foulks' for seven years, and they were described sympathetically if succinctly: 'thei be verie old, ympotent, poor and not able to paie their rents.'

In common with the rest of the kingdom, Marlow's value was assessed for taxes in 1522 and 1524 to support the King's war exchequer. Over 100 people were listed, among them Cottesmore, Sandes, Grey, Waller, Hunt, Holder, Hall, Pewsey, Tyler, Gardener, Lovejoy, Taylour, Hoker, Dene, Webb, Craford, Clerke, Beckford, Shaftesbury, Dekyn, Byrche,

Buttler, Nashe, Barnes, Robynson, Conrade, Duff, Bywaters, Saunders, Asheburne, Laurence, Williamson, Carter, Hayle, Bolde, Bothe, Johnson, Langforde, Whiteheade, Sheperde, Godfrey, Weste, Fisher, Hogson, Wyllys and Lee.

By 1674 Marlow's population was 2,394, Little Marlow 514 and Medmenham 268. In 1885 the ecclesiastical parish was enlarged, divided for civil purposes into two in 1896, one known as Marlow Urban, the other as Great Marlow, later Marlow. There were nine councillors and nine parochial church councillors.

Politically, the Claytons dominated throughout the 18th century—until Thomas Williams broke into the scene in 1790. By 1820 he owned half the town, having bought up Clayton properties. The Williams held both Marlow seats thenceforth until 1831. They organised their politics simply enough, through their tenancies. Good tenants, who voted for the Williams, did well; the less convinced were thrown out of their homes. Most of Marlow's 250 voters saw the light.

When in 1826 Londoner James Morrison challenged the Williams and polled 99 to their 128, the Williams acted—with massive evictions. Morrison aided the unfortunates, but Col William Clayton of Harleyford backed him and then, using his own substantial property power, obtained more and more votes himself until he was only four votes behind Owen Williams in 1831. With Thomas' death, the seat went to Clayton—a Reform candidate— a direct product of disgust with the system and those who exploited it, as well as with the Catholic outlook of the Williams. Clayton was Protestant.

The Reform Act which broadened the electoral base had some effect in Marlow, though less than elsewhere in the county. Some 300 voters were enlarged to 450.

In 1841 Col Clayton retained his seat by one vote, and lost it when it was discovered he had bought the vote in question. His bailiff had bribed a butcher who was in financial trouble—with some Harleyford Southdowns, having earlier refused the same man credit. Clayton was also losing the farming and trade vote, and the Williams, backed by the Wethereds, pressed the petition that unseated him, and subsequently saw their candidates back in power. The Conservatives had won; the Liberals stood no chance, in a town now favoured by wealthy families as a pleasing option to London. Almost alone in Bucks, Marlow saw little change in its representation with the wealthy in power, until the closing years of the 19th century. Other towns found middle class MPs, but even the strong 19th century dissenting vote in Marlow was insufficient to topple the powerful local landowners and employers.

Under the Redistribution of Seats Act 1885 the Borough of Marlow was merged with the county, and no more Members of Parliament sat in the Commons representing the town.

A Local Government Board Order came into operation in 1896. The effect of this eventually led to the formation of the Marlow Urban District Council. The town was known simply as Marlow in respect of postal, rail and other services, but the ecclesiastical parish still remained Great Marlow.

It was in the mid-1930s that the council offices became established at Court Garden and then on March 31, 1974, the council was wound up to be taken over by the Wycombe District Council, an amalgam of the old High Wycombe Borough Council, Marlow Urban and Wycombe Rural District Council.

Under the new system of local administration the council is a 59 seat authority with Marlow represented by five members.

Marlow began to send Members of Parliament when Edward I formed the Model Parliament. In 1301 two burghers were sent to represent the town. Their reception and what they thought of it all is lost in the mists of time, but one thing was certain, after 1307, another 300 years or more were to go by before Marlow was represented by her MPs again, when James I was king, in 1624.

Marlow eventually became a Parliamentary Borough. It consisted of the parishes of Great and Little Marlow, Medmenham, and over the river to Bisham in Berkshire. It was wholly situated within the parish of Great Marlow until 1832.

But in 1867 the number of Members returnable from Marlow was reduced to one under the provisions of the Representation of the People Act.

Following the local government re-organisation of 1974 Marlow Urban Council became a 'successor parish council'. This implied that it was in the third tier of government with the same status as a parish council.

But there was one important factor. Having been an urban council the legislation allowed such successor parish councils to opt for the name of 'Town Council'. Marlow did. And having taken that step they then agreed to have a 'Town Mayor' and 'Town Clerk'.

So Marlow's administration at the grass-roots level had gone full circle. In the days when the town was a Parliamentary Borough there was a Mayor in Marlow, even as far back as 1342.

Langley wrote: 'It has been supposed from the denomination of Chepping Marlow (which occurs in ancient records) to have been a market town at the time of the Saxons; but I find no evidence to consider it as a borough till 1299 when it was summoned to send Members to parliament by Edward the first.

'This circumstance is proof of it being a town of some consequence at that period; and yet it appears that the expence incurred by sending representatives was inconvenient to the inhabitants for they discontinued sending any after 1308; at least there are no returns existing after that date.

'There are some faint traces of a corporation, which must have been by prescription; for no charter was ever granted, as far as I can find, for this purpose. In 1342 the Mayor and Burgesses presented to the chauntry here, and continued patrons till 1394. I find no mention of these officers after this time.'

In 1681 law and order were in the hands of Little Marlow's constable George Honnor, but he appeared to be less than efficient, for he failed to pay his dues or present wrong-doers at court. John Harris, Charles Blewett, Ralph Moore and Richard Corby, overseers at Great Marlow were presented at the same court for neglect of duty—local organisation seems to have slipped somewhat. Certainly, trouble was never far beneath the surface, for John Heyward was indicted that year for assaulting Hugh Lydall and John Williams, and Joseph Gray, also of Great Marlow, was indicted for assaulting Mary Rockall. The matter had some balance—Joan Rockall, widow, Mary Corby spinster, John Plumridge and William Phillips, all of Great Marlow, were also indicted for assaulting Joseph Gray!

Next year another Honnor was in trouble. Henry Small and John Lane were accused of allowing their prisoner, William Honnor, to escape. Robert Moone was accused of being a common swearer and disturber and for speaking 'scandalous words against Mr Greene and against the Court of Sessions', and Robert Chesall failed to pay his rates—little changes.

In 1682 at Aylesbury, Marlow bargeman William Honnor pleaded guilty to stealing a saw, a case of knives, five pheasants and other items from Sir John Borlase, Bart, and the goaler was ordered to 'doe, upon Satturday next about the midd time of the day, fasten the said Honnor to the breech of a cart and strippe him naked from wast uppwards and whipp him from the Goale doore to the George signe post in Aylesbury and round the same, and soe to the Goale door againe until his body bee bloody, and soe to be dischardged, payinge his fees.'

In 1684 Richard Corby was back in trouble—for 'keepinge a dangerous Mastiff', while justice was done by Thomas Floyd, who received £4 as 'an aged and maymed souldier in his Majesties service . . . in regard he has beene ever truely loyall in his said services'. That year Marlow's constable was Thomas Lovejoy. Faced with frequently unlicensed alehouses, he understandably failed to present 'widdow' Lovejoy for her illicit trading.

Poaching was a problem: William Weedon, William Colsell, William Honnor and John Hutchens were accused in 1685 of using guns, nets and 'other engins' to destroy game. Lovejoy lost his job as petty constable, and others sworn in that year were John Herne, Abel Bird, Rumball and John Stevens. William Oxlade lost his post too, and was subsequently indicted with Richard Oxlade and Elizabeth his wife, his own wife Mary and Anne Oxlade—for assaulting the coroner, Richard Turnor.

Planning permission was flouted by John North and John East in the summer of 1685 for they were indicted for building cottages without assigning the land concerned at Marlow.

In 1686 John Law lost his job as constable, when he 'did lately siez and take into his custody out of the Crowne Inne in Greate Marlow one John Oxlade, and him did lay or sett in the Stocks in the publique markett place att or about 8 of the Clock att Night, tho itt alsoe appeared . . . that the said John Oxlade is a person of Civill life and conversation and att that tyme was not in any wise disorderly or abusive to any person, neither had he dranck one flaggon of beer'. Oxlade had brought an action for trespass against Law, so the constable had tried to get his own back.

Welfare was in mind when in 1691 the court ordered the overseers to pay £10 from the poor rate 'towards the Surgeon's Paines about the cure' of William Carter's servant. And that year Ralph Thompson, bargeman was ordered to receive £2 if he could provide a certificate showing he 'was imprest and sett on shipboard the Vanguard in the Warrs against the Dutch in the year 1666 . . . wounded in the Right Arme, Shoulder, and Cheek, and being now very impotent'. Later he received his pension.

Elizabeth Thompson of Great Marlow was before the justices in 1698 'for a common Scold, and a sedicious woman for raising and reporting false and scandelous lyes against her Neighbours', and Thomas Stapers, guilty of larceny, was ordered to be whipped at the cart's tail from Marlow market place to the signpost of the Three Tuns and back. William Phillips was presented for putting dung and straw in the road—ten cartloads of it.

Strange domestic upheavals might account for Robert Holloway's offence in 1701 when he was sent to gaol for inciting his son Robert to desert his family, while restrictive practices are certainly not new—James Blakeley, petty chapman, faced the Bench for illegally selling bone lace to William Irving, for he was not a craftsman in the trade concerned.

Eventually legislation brought about county police forces, in the 1850's. In the late 1860's drunkenness was rife in the force, and in Marlow, an inspector arrived at the Petty Sessions and treated the justices to a song, 'Marry our Margery? No! No! No!' He was sent to Padbury—back on the beat. In 1889 Marlow was one of thirteen police stations in the county.

One policeman who ended up as Deputy Chief Constable earned his laurels at Little Marlow. Supt. George Kirby worked successfully on an unusual murder case in 1922.

'Young ladies, not under 16, must be over 5ft. 6ins., well built, full figure or slim build. Required for highly paid specialised work.' So ran an advertisement to which a young lady replied on September 29. She called at George Arthur Bailey's cottage and back at home, told her father of the advertiser's unacceptable behaviour. Meanwhile Mrs Bailey had disappeared. The police were called in, and her body was found beneath her bed. Bailey had vanished. He was arrested near Reading station. Kirby was commended by the Marlow bench and by the jury.

Many years before that an attempted robbery in Marlow was solved quickly and un-usually. An Aylesbury butcher thought it might be profitable to rent a booth at Marlow Fair. After a brisk day's business he left after dark with over £80 receipts. On the road, his apprentice noticed figures ahead, and called his master, who whipped up the horse. One of the would-be thieves grabbed the tailboard of the cart.

The apprentice grabbed the first thing he could find and lashed out. It was a chopper, and next day as he cleaned the cart he found two fingers in the straw. The butcher told the police, who made enquiries at Wycombe Hospital, where they found a man receiving treatment for the rest of his injured hand.

It is not quite clear just when the first volunteers started to go about their business of putting out the inevitable fires in a town that was up to the 1600s largely composed of wood, but there is definite evidence that in the early 1700s there was a fire engine in Marlow and it was garaged in the porch of the original parish church—opposite the 'Dead House'.

Whether it was the first engine or not is uncertain, but today, beautifully restored and in working order is a hand-operated machine that was the gift of John Clavering, Esq., 'To the Borough of Great Marlow, 1731'. It is obvious that this machine at least was parked in the first church porch as it was not until 1832 that the second church was built.

In 1807 there was no mention made of a fire engine, but later the machine was garaged at the Town Hall, adjacent to the Town lock-up. It was a manually-operated pump drawn by horses. Now the horses could not be kept permanently in the station so they were allowed to graze in a field at the rear of the Town Hall and Crown Hotel, which is now the Riley Recreation open space.

Needless to say when an alarm call was received—and this was usually by someone standing ringing the bell outside the Town Hall 'for five minutes or until the firemen arrive' —there was all sorts of comedy as the horses had to be caught and harnessed up.

When this was finally achieved the firemen would go off at a gallop followed by almost every small boy in Marlow. Arriving at the fire the manual pump had to be worked with firemen on either side of the machine holding on to a kind of parallel-bars arrangement. When they were exhausted the boys took over. They gave in their names and any boy whose name appeared on a list later posted outside the Crown could claim half-a-crown for his labours.

Sometimes the fire engine horses earned their keep and there is a tale passed on within one family that one Beckett of South Plain had the horses pulling a bus. Anyone leaving their name at the Crown Hotel would be called for and taken to the railway station with their baggage for 6d (sixpence). If, unhappily, the fire bells were heard while on the way to the station, the horses were unharnessed and Beckett, riding one and leading the other, would gallop off to the fire station leaving the 'fares' to fend for themselves.

Between the wars the firemen decided to dispense with the horses. An old Daimler car was purchased from Mrs Taylor of Stoneyware, Bisham, and connected to the manual. The arrangement was not entirely satisfactory so it was decided to buy a 'custom-built' fire appliance. The Daimler car was converted to an ambulance which went on to give good service in the area for years after.

ABOVE: In 1896 Marlow UDC was formed and replaced these
Great Marlow Parish Councillors.

BELOW: The officers and members of the last UDC—eliminated in 1974's
countrywide reorganisation of local government.

ABOVE: Court Garden, home to the Council from the early 1930s.

CENTRE: The sports and leisure complex at Court Garden.

BELOW: Victim of the planners—a Spittal Square shop
built and demolished within six years.

To the Electors of the
BOROUGH OF GREAT MARLOW,
AND THE
PARISHES OF LITTLE MARLOW, MEDMENHAM, AND BISHAM.

GENTLEMEN,

After the long and intimate connection of myself (and those of my family who have preceded me) with the Borough of Great Marlow, it is with deep regret I find myself called upon to address you with reference to its severance.

I do not take this step without due consideration and on the advice of those Gentlemen composing my Committee, whose opinions I am bound to respect and adopt, and as they deem a close and continuous canvass up to the dissolution imperative, I confess I do not feel equal to so arduous an undertaking, added to the fact that, having represented the Borough for a period near upon half a century, my political principles must be well known to the bulk of the constituency.

It is, however, highly gratifying to be enabled to state that the result of my canvass has been satisfactory, as far as it went, and I have no doubt that if carried to a poll it would have proved successful.

I trust that in resigning my charge into your hands that in your selection of a Candidate to supply my place you will remember the interests of the nation at large, and that the principles, of whomsover you may think proper to select, may be in accordance with the preservation intact of the great National Institutions both in Church and State, and as I believe the great majority of your constituency to be strongly conservative, I sincerely hope you will return a Member whose political views are coincident.

And now, with feelings of the deepest gratitude to those who have so handsomely promised me their support, as well as to the many staunch and generous friends who have, for so many years, adhered to my interests, I heartily and sincerely bid you farewell,

And remain,

GENTLEMEN,

Your obliged and faithful Servant,

THOMAS PEERS WILLIAMS.

TEMPLE HOUSE,
October 15th, 1868.

W. BURNHAM, PRINTER, MAIDENHEAD.

MA
ELECTIO
Respectfully ded
E. H. VERNEY, E
AIR.---".*All the Blue*

March ! March ! Marlow and Bisham Men !
See how our ranks gather deeper and broader.
Poll ; Poll ! High Street and Chapel Street !
All the Blue Voters are lost in disorder !
Come, jolly Working Men,
Never to Shirking Men !
Leave Shop and Counting House, Kitchen and Parlour,
Never a better Head
Led us than WETHERED :
Ho ! for the House that is famous in Marlow !
Then March ! March ! Marlow and Bisham Men !
See how our ranks thicken, deeper and broader.
Never a better Head led us than WETHERED !
All the Blue Voters are gone to disorder !

Come ! Come ! West Street and Peter's Street ;
Well-Enders, Lane-Enders, all other Enders :
Boaters and Cricketers, Bargemen and Fishermen,
Yeomanry, Riflemen, all our Defenders .
Mill-hands and Shoe-hands,
And Farm-hands and Brew-hands ;
All who are thriving by brave honest labour ;
Back the good fellow, who
Labours along with you ;
Poll for TOM WETHERED, Townsman, and Neighbour !
So March ! March ! Little Marlow and Medmenham !
Watch the ranks ! How they swell ! closer and broa
Never a better Head led us than WETHERED !
All the Blue voters are lost in disorder !

Hark to the Blues, and the language they scream at us,
" Perfidy---Treason---Coercion "---and stuff !
Free is your Conscience, nor cares for their nonsense ;
Free are we all, and the thought is enough !
No Master Verney,
We'll never return ye !
Strangers have led us too long, of a truth,
What ! again take a stranger ?
Another ?---No danger !
Hail to the Friend who was ours from his youth !
Then March ! March ! Marlows and Medmenham !
Verney's abuse becomes coarser and broader ;
Never a better Head led us than WETHERED !
All the Blue voters may go to disorder !

BURNHAM,

LOW

MARCH,

(...out permission) to

...OMMANDER, R.N.

...are over the Border."

...ho! who! got up our Cricket Club,
  Laid down its turf, and laid down its rules?
...hose activity started our Riflemen?
  Whose liberality built us our Schools?
    Who will abet us,
    Our Railway to get us?
...ho feed the weak, and find work for the strong?
    Who feel with all of us,
    Great, middle, small of us?
...ETHEREDS and WETHEREDS for ever so long!
  Then March! Marlow and Bisham men!
    Room in the ranks there! Deeper and Broader!
  Poll! Poll! Lane End and Flackwell Heath!
    All the Blue voters are fled without order!

...rney would leave the old Country defenceless,—
  Blow up the Church from the steps to the steeple,—
...ing up our wee things as outcasts and heathens,—
    That's his idea of the Rights of the People!
    Give us the Champion, who
    Knows how our wishes go,
...elps the true purpose, the honest endeavour!
    Progress and Liberty,
    Flourish with such as he;
...ETHERED's the man for us! WETHERED for ever!
  Then March! Marlows and Medmenham,
    Verney is plying hard words and soft sawder.
  Poll! Poll! Bisham and Flackwell Heath!
    All the Blue Policy leads to Disorder!

...te! Vote! Free men and Honest men!
  Careless of humbug, and quibbles bewild'ring,
...ng from the Steeple the Choice of the People,
  WETHERED for MARLOW, for HOME, WIFE and CHILDREN!
    Up with the Orange Flag!
    See how the blue shall lag!
...rney shall find his hope sunk, and his star low.
    Fill up the Muster-roll!
    Orange shall head the Poll!
...eer! my boys, Cheer! for TOM WETHERED and MARLOW,
  Then Poll! Poll! Brave men and Honest men!
    Spread the ranks! Swell the ranks! Deeper and broader,
  Never a better Head led us than WETHERED!
    Orange to Victory! Blue to Disorder!

...IDENHEAD.

...ndly in the 19th century.

...al, originally in Cambridge
...ived 1970 closure plans.

...r the elderly on the site of
...emolished 1969).

TO THE

WORKING MEN

OF THE BOROUGH OF

GREAT MARLOW.

FELLOW WORKMEN,

We have been talking a deal amongst ourselves lately, about this coming Election, and it seems to me that some of us do not understand what we are going to vote about, and what with one thing and another, I am sure some of us wish we had nothing to do with it at all. But still after all, the Vote we have got is a sort of trust, and as we have got it, it is our duty of course to use it for our own good and the Country, and so, Fellow-Workmen, I have been thinking the matter out, and this is what it comes to in my mind.

After all, the question is not what any of us have said to Captain VERNEY, when Colonel WILLIAMS was standing, that has got nothing to do with it; but what we ought to do *now*, now a new man has come forward. Let the other side say what they please, Captain VERNEY against Mr. WETHERED, is not the same thing at all as Captain VERNEY against Colonel WILLIAMS, and it is against all honesty and common sense to think so; for if we took one man's part against another, it does not follow we must take that man's part against everybody else. Most of those of us who took the Captain's part, thought that he was a better man than Colonel Williams, because the Colonel never had done much for us, or for the trade of the place, or in Parliament either for that matter, and we told him so. But when Mr. WETHERED came forward, we saw there was a man we knew, who was a working man amongst us, who was not a stranger to us, who has done a deal of good for the place, and whose interests are the same as ours; and from always living among us, and taking a part in all we do, such a man I think must know and feel our wants better than a stranger, and be more likely to represent us as we want to be in Parliament.

If any man thinks that Captain Verney is the best man still, in God's name let that man vote to his liking, but for my part, whatever I have said before, when Colonel Williams was standing, I shall vote boldly and honestly, for the man I think the best man, and who will do us the most good, and as the Captain says he wants us to vote according to our conscience, I think our consciences will be best satisfied if we vote for Mr. WETHERED.

A WORKING MAN.

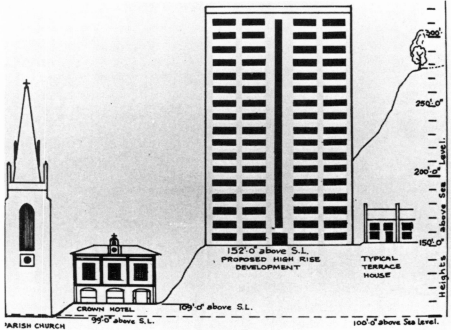

ABOVE LEFT: This balloon sailed 200 ft above the town when
the planners showed Marlow what 'high rise' would mean, in 1967.

BELOW: Marlow Society's warning to the town—this was
their view of the Council's 'high rise' development.
It never happened, and four storeys are the limit today.

ABOVE RIGHT: John Brinkhurst's 1608 almshouses in
Oxford lane end their days, 361 years later.

90

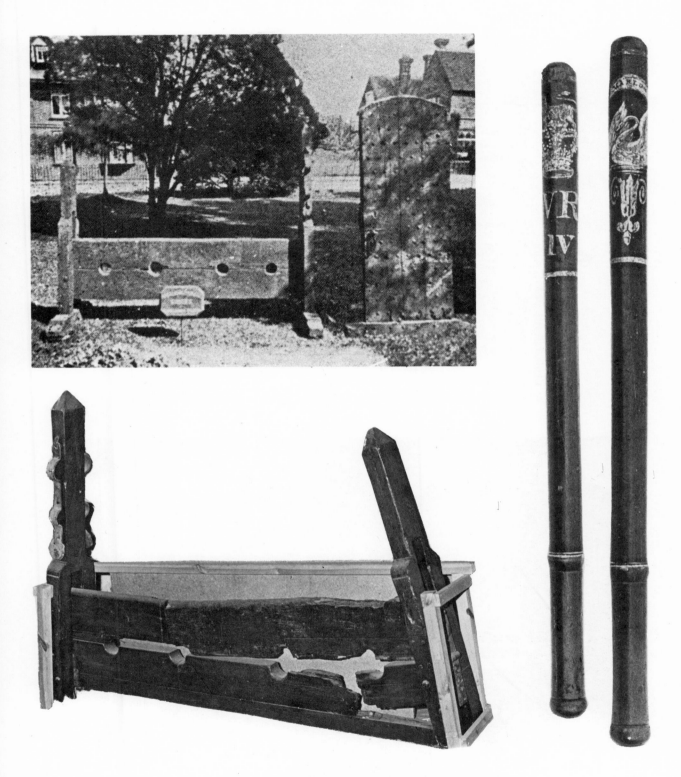

ABOVE : 1876 was the last time the stocks were in use in Market Place. They went to The Causeway, together with a cell-door from the town lock-up.

BELOW : Marlow's stocks still survive—at Bucks County Museum.

RIGHT : Marlow's parish constable's baton dates from the reign of William IV. It depicts Marlow's swan, and the crown.

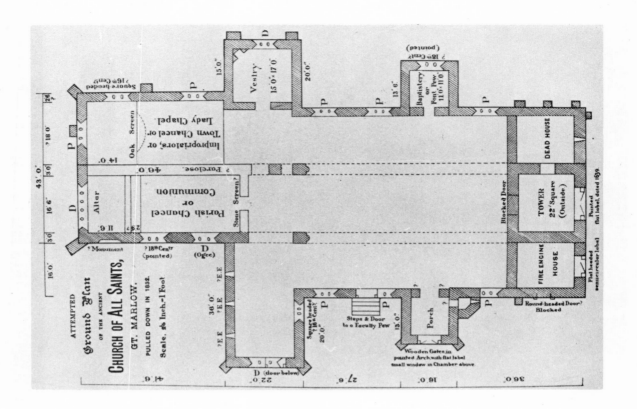

ABOVE: The Parish Church once housed the fire engine; this plan shows where.

BELOW: Vera was the first petrol driven fire appliance in 1920.

The 1731 fire engine is still at the Cambridge Road fire station.

ABOVE: The Grammar School, from an old print.

An 1880 early photograph of the original Borlase
building and adjoining homes.

BELOW: Borlase School football team, after playing to raise
Cottage Hospital funds—several of these players joined the town team.

94

Much in Mind

Over three-and-a-half centuries ago, in 1624, Sir William Borlase founded the school in West Street, which to this day still bears his name. John Borlace (the original spelling) was from an old Cornish family tracing its descent to Norman times. In Elizabethan days John bought the manor of Little Marlow and was both sheriff and MP for Buckinghamshire.

His son William founded the school as a memorial to his son Henry, MP for Marlow. To fund the venture he bought a farm at Bix and cottages in Chapel Street.

The Will of Sir William set out the tenets he wished to be followed. Twelve pupils whose parents were too poor to pay for their education were to be admitted annually and taught to 'read, write and cast accounts' for two years. They were then expected to be fitted to become apprentices when they were to be paid 40 shillings to bind them legally.

To this day the school mottoes can be seen on the walls of the school. They are quotations from the new Authorised Version of the Bible published in 1611. They read: 'If any will not worke neither shall he eate. 2 Thessa 3. 10', and 'In the sweate of thy face shalt thou eate bread. Genesis 3. 19'.

Hugh Tanner, under the terms of the Will, was to occupy a cottage on the west side of the School and was to 'teach 24 poor women's children to make bone lace, spin or knit.' He was also to whip such delinquents as were brought to him by petty constables, Churchwardens, overseers and tithing men.

The Education Act of 1870 had a profound effect. There were plenty of schools in Marlow to deal with the new situation. Seven years after the Act the Feoffees felt that Borlase had completed its mission for teaching the 'three Rs' and they decided to turn it into a grammar school.

Newly appointed Headmaster, the Rev Michael Graves, later Canon Graves, started literally from scratch—no school, no staff and no pupils. Being a resourceful man he bought some iron sheds and built a new west wing on the site of the old House of Correction. There were soon over 100 boarders and the town had to be scoured for accommodation. It was found at Kentons in Glade Road; at the top of High Street where the International Stores used to be and the Old House in West Street.

Borlase was now a public school. The County Councils Act of 1881 meant education was taken over by Buckinghamshire County Council and so it has remained to the present day. Boarding is now at Sentry Hill only and over 500 boys are on the school roll.

St Peter's Roman Catholic School recently moved to Prospect Road. It was in St Peter Street prior to that and sprang from a free school started by Mr Scott Murray of Danesfield. He persuaded the Sisters of St Paul in Birmingham to open the first establishment in Albion House, 26 years after the poet Shelley had vacated the property. Later a convent and school were built next to the Pugin Church in St Peter Street.

The Church of England had several schools under their control for a time, in Oxford

Road and St Peter Street. There was also the former Boys' School at The Causeway or Church Passage, which in 1913 moved to a new building in Wethered Road, known today as Holy Trinity School.

Until 1961 this had been a secondary school, but in that year Great Marlow School was opened for secondary pupils, leaving Holy Trinity as a 'middle' school.

There was also rapid progress at Foxes Piece in the late 1960s where the initial Infants School became a 'first' school and in 1969 a separate middle school was added to the site.

Marlow Bottom has its own Burford School, and Danesfield School that started life as a black corrugated coagulation of sheds under the trees of Razzler Woods, is now a permanent brick building, taking in numerous children from the town of Marlow, though its first purpose was for the children of servicemen at RAF Medmenham.

In 1968 a new wall and gate enclosed the school.

ABOVE LEFT: The school insignia—based on the Borlase crest.

ABOVE RIGHT: Church Hall at The Causeway,
the Boys' School until 1913.

BELOW: Wethered Road School, the post-1913 replacement of the Church
Hall, renamed Holy Trinity when the secondary school
moved to Bobmore Lane.

97

ABOVE: Gen Sir George Higginson founded a school at
Bovingdon Green, now closed: scholars in 1919.

CENTRE: Dial Close School, established in The Causeway in 1929, closed
in 1972: final speechday at Borlase School gymnasium.

BELOW: Great Marlow school.

Behind the Lines

Although Marlow and the surrounding district was an important centre commercially and from a communications point of view, there was never anything vital about its strategic situation in any of the wars that have rent England.

Even the most hostile of all the invaders who passed across the area, the Danes, avoided pitched battles in the district. They did establish a fortified encampment at Danesfield, though no records exist to show how they were eventually ousted from their ancient stronghold.

There is no record of any significant conflict following the Saxons or Normans into Marlow, and no proof that the Wars of the Roses had any great impact. But when Charles I imposed his infamous Ship Money tax in inland towns, Marlow did not escape the net. Sheriff Temple first asked the authorities if he was to assess the town separately or as part of its hundred. Apparently Marlow's earlier lack of parliamentary representation and 1624 reinstatement made it an administratively grey area. It was one of three Bucks towns in this position.

High Constable of Marlow was Robert Chace; the Chaces of Marlow were related to Chesham's Matthew Chace who founded the American dynasty that established the Chase Manhattan Bank. Chace squeezed precisely 8s out of the town in 1635.

Some Marlow landowners were assessed highly on their worth: John Borlace was put down at a value of £3,000. He was ward of the king's woods in Radnage, Great Marlow and Medmenham. In 1636 he had not paid his tax—11s 4d. But Lord and Lady Powes did pay 12s, and Richard Langley 6d. Roberte Brandon undertook to collect outstanding monies from outside the town—£6 13s.

In 1637 Richard Grenville noted that Marlow was taxed £51, and that in 1640 the town yielded £15 10s 6d, while the district around produced £25 14s and Little Marlow £16 3s 7d. There is no record of any complaint by Marlovians, but they may have decided to lay low and pay up, for the Civil War was imminent, and the town was not notable for its enthusiasm for parliament or nonconformity.

During the Civil War Major General Brown entered Marlow and he garrisoned his troops in the Parish Church. The only incident recorded at that time was the damage to the then-Marlow Bridge.

In 1693 a foot soldier marching from Beaconsfield to Marlow accidentally fired his gun, damaging his hand. He lay sick at Marlow for some weeks and Marlow claimed the cost of the surgeon's fees.

Seventeenth and eighteenth century court records show that local men were pressed into military service with little compunction.

In the 19th century there was civil violence in the streets on two occasions when rioting broke out following the declaration of an election result.

This was 1880. Fighting broke out generally when the result was declared and as the running battle gained momentum one window at Wethered's offices was smashed by a missile. This was the trigger for even more violence and damage to property. There was hardly a window left in the brewery offices before long and then the targets became the Town Hall itself, and the adjacent Crown Hotel. Again many windows were shattered and there was even a dent in the town clock face!

Police were far outnumbered and a call for help was sent to Windsor Barracks for troops. But there was no response as the request had not been signed by a magistrate.

As the rumpus began to subside the police swooped and succeeded in rounding up the ringleaders, promptly throwing them in the town lock-up, (a cell under the Crown).

A local bookmaker, Jack Langley, who was a bit of a card in his day, and lived at various times at Caldwell Lodge, The Rookery, New Court and Old Bridge House, mounted a rescue operation. The imprisoned ringleaders stayed imprisoned, and Langley was caught. He was sentenced to six weeks' jail for his part in the affair but when he was released he received an inscribed silver salver recognising his courage by 'some sympathisers'.

In 1834 Sir William Clayton was behind the formation of the Royal Bucks Yeomanry, which ultimately became the Royal Bucks Hussars. Some years before that there had been another strong military tie in the town. The Royal Military Academy, then based in High Wycombe had a Junior Department at Marlow housed in 'Remnantz'. This unit was there from 1802 until 1812 after which everything was moved to Blackwater and was destined to become Sandhurst. Marlow Place was a royal residence and George III spent some time at the Academy while it was in Marlow.

The cadets at Remnantz were aged from 13 to 17. By 1803 there were 400 at the College. Free education was offered to 100 sons of officers killed in action; eighty sons of serving officers were to pay £40 a year; a hundred sons of nobility were offered places; and sixty Royal Artillery cadets as well as sixty intended for the East India Company would each pay £90 a year. Marlow Place was obtained to house the overflow.

At 5 am the drums sounded and at six came parade and inspection. Prayers followed with study at seven and breakfast at nine. At 10—more study, then 'fencing, riding, swimming and the sabre' with dinner at two. More study at three, military exercises at 5.30, supper at 8.30 and after prayers, to bed at 10. Recreation was allowed two short periods during each day.

Despite the intention behind Marlow to secure officers of merit, the Army for many years chose officers of existing social rank. Few Marlow cadets achieved fame, except perhaps Somers Cocks, of whom Wellington said at his funeral—'If Cocks had lived, which was a moral impossibility, since he exposed himself too much to risks, he would have been one of the greatest generals we ever had.'

The College saw its share of trouble. In 1804 there was mutiny—nine cadets set up a plan of arson and armed attack to force the dismissal of an unpopular commander. They failed. They were expelled publicly. The King regarded the College as of 'the deepest national importance'. Still, cadets scrawled slogans on the walls of Remnantz. The staff complained for more money for long hours. In 1810 another cadet was expelled for a rebellious pamphlet. In 1812 the cadets started to leave, for Sandhurst was ready for them.

Perhaps the most romantic war story of all concerns a horse. 'Skirmisher' was ridden as a charger by Colonel Sir William Robert Clayton throughout the Peninsula War and in subsequent campaigns in the Netherlands. The great black beast was at Waterloo in 1815 but was fatally wounded in the advance on Paris.

Such was the attachment between man and horse that Sir William had the body of the charger brought back to Marlow where it was laid to rest in 'Colonel's Meadow' in the grounds of Sir William Borlase's School.

A tablet commemorating 'Skirmisher' and his exploits was set up in the wall of a garden near a cottage at that time. Later the stone was removed and re-established in the grounds of Harleyford Manor, the Clayton family seat. The regard for 'Skirmisher' may be judged from the verses compiled by Sir William:

'Sleep on, Sleep on, Thou faithful one,
Light lie the turf upon thy Breast,
Thy toil is o'er thy race is run,
Sleep on and take thy rest.
In vain for thee were the 'Larum Note,
Pour'd from the bugle's brazen throat,
The rolling drum thou heedest not,
        Nor noise of signal gun.
Let Charger tramp and Warrior tread
Over the place of thy narrow bed,
They will not wake thee from the dead,
        Thy Mortal Strife is Done.
Sleep on, Sleep on, No morrow's sun
Shall light thee to the battle back,
The fight is closed, thy Laurels won,
        And this thy Bivouac.
On tented field, or Bloody Plain,
For thee the watch fire flares in vain,
Thou wilt not share its warmth again,
        With him who loved thee well.'

Also inscribed is: 'Here is buried Skirmisher, Aged 24 years. Rode by Colonel Sir William Robert Clayton, Bart, as a Charger During the Arduous Campaign in Spain and Portugal, 1812 and 1813. And at the Battles of Vottoria, six Days Actions at the Pyrenees, Crossing the Dour, before Pampeluna and in the pursuit of the Divisions of Marshal Lucket, in the advance on Salamanca. Also during the campaign in the Netherlands, and at the field of Quatre Bras, June 16. The Battle of Genappe, June 17 and Waterloo, June 18, 1815. In which two last engagements the Horse was twice wounded by Shot and Shell in the Advance on Paris and subsequent capitulation in 1815.'

In the 20th century Marlow was once again little affected by the strife of a trouble-torn world. In the first world war the Royal Engineers arrived in town to train in the digging and revetting of trenches. Many of the earthworks remain to this day at Marlow Common and are still known as 'The Trenches'.

As the Kaiser's war escalated there were numerous recruiting campaigns carried out, mostly in Market Square. And while soldiers arrived to train, local boys marched off to the front, having already served with the Territorials. Some of them marched off to Wooburn on the actual day of the declaration—August 4, 1914.

History was to repeat itself on September 3, 1939, when the Oxon and Bucks Light Infantry Territorials also marched up High Street for Wooburn. The second world war came a lot nearer home as civilians were placed in the firing line due to advances in aviation.

So it was in mid-1940, just as the Battle of Britain was intensifying, that British fighters tore into formations of German bombers to the west of Marlow. The invaders opted to jettison their cargoes of death and make for home.

An estimated 150 bombs crashed down over fields and meadows to the west of the town. There was slight damage to Western House and little else. But the incident brought Marlow its first war casualty, and as it turned out the only one in the town. The fatally wounded victim is commemorated by street name—off Oxford Road, at Ryan's Mount. There was one more incident before peace arrived.

It was on July 22, 1944, that Marlow witnessed the appearance of a 'Doodlebug', or V1. Today Jim Platt is the managing-director of a busy and successful garage business in Marlow, but the day the 'doodlebug' arrived could well have been his last. He was visiting his grandmother at her home in Bovingdon Green when it arrived. It struck some trees nearby, so minimising damage to the house. Mr Platt, then only a lad of 10, was severely injured by flying fragments, but recovered.

Just as German bombs falling on Greenwich brought one of the first industrial companies to Marlow during the war when the sawmills were bombed out in London, so did a German bomb bring one of the most vital and important units of the Royal Air Force to the district.

The bomb fell on Croydon. It completely wiped out the equipment of the unit working on aerial reconnaissance interpretation. The Air Ministry searched quickly for a suitable site to re-establish the unit and settled eventually on Danesfield House.

Situated within easy driving distance of Benson airfield the unit at Medmenham pored over thousands of mosaics brought back by unarmed, high-flying aircraft from enemy territory. It was at Medmenham that the existence of the flying-bomb or V1 first became known to the Allies. From aerial photographs taken over the Rhur, models were prepared to aid the famous 'Dam Busters' to carry out their brilliant raid on the dams of the Eder, Moene and Sorpe. The unit eventually closed down in 1964, the last act being the burning of 150 tons of photographs.

There was another historic occasion at the station which is headquarters of the RAF Signals Command, in March 1970. This was when the 'Gee' navigational system was finally closed down. 'Gee' was a radio aid developed during the war to help Bomber Command's air offence become more effective. The system was continued in the years of peace immediately after the war but options were taken up on other systems and so there was a 'symbolic' closing down of the chain that had operated without pause for 28 years. The RAF unit at Medmenham is now expected to close in 1977.

ABOVE: 1500 spearhead, recovered from the Thames.
(Bucks County Museum.)

Successors to the Yeomanry—
the Royal Bucks Hussars.

BELOW RIGHT: Sir William Clayton, Commander of the
Royal Bucks Yeomanry.

BELOW LEFT: Memorial to the famous charger, Skirmisher.

ABOVE LEFT: Civil commotion in Marlow in 1880, when election riots modified the glazing of Town Hall and Crown.

ABOVE RIGHT: The mob also showed their disapproval of the Election result, at Marlow Brewery's headquarters.

BELOW LEFT: World War I trainees come to Marlow; some stationed at Spinfield learnt trenching on Marlow Common.

BELOW RIGHT: Market Square was Marlow's recruitment base.

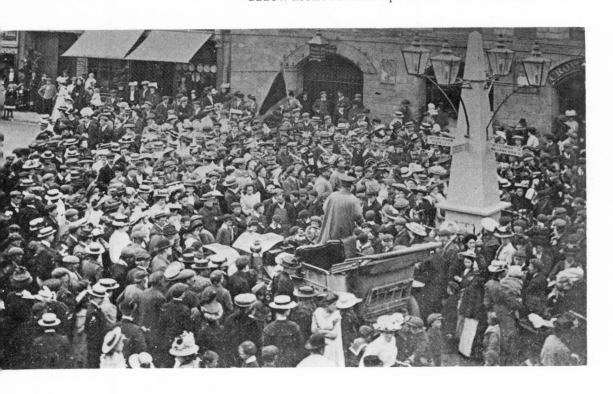

ABOVE: Marlow men prepare to leave for the '14-18 front.

CENTRE: Gen Sir George Higginson, of Gyldernscroft,
inspects Royal Engineers after local training.

BELOW: September 3, 1939 and Marlow Territorial Army
men march to Wooburn.

106

ABOVE: September 3, 1939. Marlow & Wooburn Company, Oxon and Bucks Light Infantry immediately prior to embarkation for France.

BELOW: Marlow Place, once part of the Royal Military College 1802-1812, was a 'shadow factory' in World War II.

ABOVE: Remembrance Day at The Causeway.

BELOW: Jim Platt, survivor of injuries from a World War II
flying bomb that landed on Marlow when he was 10.

ABOVE: Danesfield House, officers' mess at RAF Medmenham, home of
the wartime navigational aid, 'Gee' and open to the public
only once—in September 1975.

BELOW: Theodore Lunnon of Marlow (1939-45 DSM),
later OC (Marlow's) Training Ship Snipe, now renamed Apollo.

ABOVE LEFT: Mary Shelly wrote Frankenstein while in Marlow.

ABOVE RIGHT: Percy Bysshe Shelley (1792-1822), poet
who came to Marlow for three years. (Both Mansell Collection).

BELOW: The Shelleys' home in West Street, as it once was.

Glittering Grass

World-famous names in literature and art, theatre and architecture have been connected with Marlow in its time. The poet Percy Bysshe Shelley once lived in the town, attracting a number of other well-known writers of the day. At Quarry Wood Hall in Edwardian England, many household names of the day spent their leisure hours appreciating the beauties of the district.

The best-known personality was Shelley, yet his association with the town was not of any great duration—only three years. Thomas Love Peacock, himself an established writer of the day, was responsible for bringing his friend Shelley to Marlow as it was Peacock who found Albion House, adjacent to Borlase school.

That was in February 1817. While in Marlow Shelley wrote 'Revolt of Islam'. His wife, Mary was also busy writing, and eventually produced the classic 'Frankenstein'.

Shelley was 24 when he came to Marlow. Mary was his second wife, and the daughter of Godwin, the Apostle of Liberty. Also in Albion House were Claire Clairmont, the daughter of Godwin's wife by a former marriage, and her child Allegra, an illegitimate daughter of Lord Byron. Visitors to the Shelley household included Leigh Hunt, then editor of 'The Examiner' and Thomas Jefferson Hogg, who had been rusticated from Oxford with Shelley.

Shelley endeared himself to many Marlow people in the brief time he was in the town. Tales were told of how he gave away his clothes to the poor and in the middle of winter would distribute blankets among his neighbours in West Street. But there was one person with whom Shelley could not get on—William Francis, the Headmaster at Borlase School. In the dedication to his 'Revolt of Islam', Shelley wrote a verse that seems to indicate what he thought of his neighbours:

> 'I do remember well the hour that burst
> My spirit's sleep; a fresh May morn it was,
> When I walked forth upon the glittering grass,
> And wept, I knew not why; until there rose
> From the near schoolroom, voices, that alas!
> Were but one echo from the world of woes—
> The harsh and grating strife of tyrants and of foes.'

In her 'Preface to Shelley's Poems', Mary wrote: 'The poem (Revolt of Islam) was written in his boat as it floated under the beech groves of Bisham, or during wanderings in the neighbouring country which is distinguished by peculiar beauty. The chalk hills break into cliffs that overhang the Thames, or form valleys clothed with beech; the wilder portion of the country is rendered beautiful by exuberant vegetation; and the cultivated part is particularly fertile.'

In the same preface, Mrs Shelley gives a rather startling and stark picture of the lot of the people in those days: 'With all this wealth of nature which, either in the form of gentle-

111

men's parks, or soil dedicated to agriculture, flourishes around, Marlow was inhabited by a very poor population. The women were lace-makers and lost their health by sedentary labour, for which they were ill-paid.'

Jerome J. Jerome, author of 'Three Men in a Boat', had even stronger and longer local connections than Shelley. Around 1910 he moved into Monks Corner, a house at Marlow Common, which was built at the beginning of the century by Conrad Dressler. Sculptor Dressler was a naturalised Austrian, responsible for the 'delle Robbia' frieze around the entrance. He also had a small kiln and produced hand-made 'Medmenham' tiles, which at that time were in vogue.

Jerome had lived, prior to moving to Monks Corner, at Wood End House and he stayed 10 years before moving in 1920 to Ridge End—a cottage that he had enlarged. His book 'They and I' was written with this background.

Another local man of letters was G. P. R. James. Now there is little recognition of his works, but in the 19th century he was among the most popular writers of his time. He resided at 'Quoitings', Oxford Road in the 1830s. His father had been a doctor, on occasion tending George IV. He held the position of Historiographer Royal to both William IV and Queen Victoria. In all he wrote about 90 political, romantic and historical novels as well as having published some histories and biographies, in 1838 writing what was at that time the standard work on the life of Louis XIV.

In the church there is a picture of 'The Piebald Boy'. The painting is the work of Coventry in 1811. Showman John Richardson who was born in the Workhouse at Marlow bought the boy, a native of the Caribbean Islands for 1,000 guineas.

Richardson christened the boy 'George Alexander Gratton'. The picture shows the boy with his dog. The child died in 1813, probably succumbing to the English climate but not before Richardson had exhibited his find in many parts of the country. Aged four years and nine months when he died, Richardson had him interred in a vault on the north side of the Churchyard.

On his own death in 1836 Richardson was buried in the same vault and two headstones, back to back, mark the tomb. There is an inscription on the child's last resting place.
Included in this are the lines:

> 'Know that beneath this humble stone
> A child of colour, haply not thine own
> This parents born of Afric's sun burnt race.
> The white and black were blended in his face
> To Britain brought, which made his parents free,
> And showed the world great nature's prodigy'.

A tangible reminder of a well-known theatre impresario, Charles Frohman, stands at The Causeway. He never actually carried out any of his stage-work in the area, but 'loved Marlow better than any place in the world'. American-born Frohman died when the 'Lusitania' was torpedoed on May 7, 1915. The memorial, which was a drinking fountain when it was first erected, takes the form of a nude lady. The figure was modelled by a local woman and the sculptor responsible for the design and completed work was Leonard S. Merrifield. Round the base of the monument runs the following inscription: 'For it is not right that in a house the Muses haunt, mourning should dwell; such things befit us not'.

Believed to stand on the site of a former Saxon settlement at the foot of Quarry Woods, Quarry Wood Hall was built in 1901 from a design by Aubrey Beardsley; the hall is the most complete and authentic example of Edwardian Gothic architecture in England.

Dame Nellie Melba stayed there and local people would take to their boats to listen to her beautiful voice as she rehearsed. Providing there was no applause she would sing song after song. In the 1920s, vivacious steel heiress Mrs Laura Corrigan from Cleveland, Ohio, leased the house. A hostess of renown she was responsible for a host of personalities and 'bright young things' being in the area at week-ends.

A delightfully graphic account of the goings on has been written by Lance Arundell: 'Marlovians taking an innocent stroll on the opposite bank would, at one time or another, be amused by some delightful sights. Tallulah Bankhead and Lord Arlington demonstrating "The Shimmy" to the accompaniment of an all-Negro band while the Sitwells recited poetry to Augustus John's bulldog; Lady Diana Duff Cooper and Virginia Woolf were huddling at easels, painting each other's portraits, while the Queen of Spain, Elinor Glyn and the Grand Duchess of Russia evoked the spirits with a seance; Nancy Mitford was playing croquet on the great lawn with Evelyn Waugh and Lord Weymouth, while Scott and Zelda Fitzgerald nibbled muffins with Princess San Ferdinando and her two pet cheetahs on a leash.

'Noel Coward was inspired to write "Hay Fever" and Lady Eleanor Smith and Loelia Ponsonby would race through the village at dawn on one of their treasure hunts. A group of Marlow boy scouts, creeping down Winter Hill, were startled to come across Isadora Duncan, in a glade of the Woods, creating her celebrated "Dance of the Wood Nymph". There was a constant coming and going of the avante garde and when Mrs Corrigan bade Marlow farewell, the villagers watched her departure with very mixed feelings indeed.'

Quarry Wood Hall later fell sadly into disrepair but was bought by Henry James Tilt with a view to it being restored and to house his art collection. The second world war intervened, and the hall was used to shelter tenants from Mr Tilt's bombed-out Dulwich estate.

After the war Mr Tilt and his daughter, Mrs Constance Harvey restored the hall to its original glory. It is now owned by Mr Tilt's grand-daughter and is lived in by his grandson, Mr Henry Clayton. A striking stained-glass window in Quarry Wood Hall, the work of William Morris, depicts Queen Maud's son, Henry II, killing a wild boar.

Artistic pursuits have always been encouraged in the Marlow area. The Marlow Art and Crafts Society run successful exhibitions, and the oldest dramatic group in the town is the Amateur Operatic Society, who have a long history of devotion to Gilbert and Sullivan operas. Their first performance was in 1920—'HMS Pinafore'.

There have been numerous remarkable people in the Bovingdon Green and Marlow Common areas. In 1912 A. L. Baldry, the art critic and artist in pastels, built Wolmer Wood, a house to be lived in much later by a former Borlase boy and television star, Paul Daneman. Baldry was a regular contributor to 'The Studio' in his day. Then at Lord's Wood lived Mrs Sergeant Florence, a distinguished designer of fresco work and the author of a standard work on the subject. She was often to be seen striding up from Marlow Station to the Common after a day in London, with a bundle over her shoulder.

Finally, there was a gentleman who resided near the top of High Street. His fiancee died before they got married and as a keepsake of his courtship he wore one of her teeth mounted on a tie-pin. History does not reveal whether he ever did marry.

The river gave rise to more than poignant parties and poetry. In 1892, Alfred Heneage Cocks wrote of his youth earlier in the century, when the river was haunted by bargees, professional fishermen and parties from London, following Izaak Walton's recommendations. They hired punts by the day, together with a fisherman. But by 1892 Cocks saw 'odious steam launches' and thousands of tourists on the waters; barges were virtually non-existent. So he listed some of the local words he had heard in general use in Marlow, and which were gradually disappearing from local vocabularies.

They included these: athirt for across, backer for thrash ('I'll give him backer'); dawsey for drowsy; drucksey for unsound (sic. wood); dumb-dollie for posts across a footpath to exclude vehicles; fagot—a contemptuous term for a woman; gallus for very; neestie for nest; peckid for pointed; scuffle-hunter for a freshwater stevedore; to stag, for to watch for (the foreman); titter-totter for see-saw; unked for uncouth; wum for a ripple and cheese-log for a woodlouse.

A strange tale is said by some to have originated in the old 'Barge Pole' or the Medmenham Hotel: the landlady noticed that her larder was being depleted. After careful observation and thought she discovered that bargees were responsible. So to teach them a lesson they would never forget she prepared a special pie and casually laid it on a window sill to cool. It disappeared according to plan.

Whoever the aggrieved was, she informed the thieving bargees from the heights of Marlow bridge of the contents of the pie: recently drowned puppies.

It was thereafter considered great sport by the young blades of the town to taunt bargees plying their craft up and down the Thames with the words: 'Who ate puppy pie under Marlow Bridge?'. But the person who was brave—or stupid—enough to shout this abuse had also to be a good sprinter.

There was one flamboyant character though who didn't give a jot for the possible consequences . . . Captain Marshall. He was a figure of some interest in the town centre on shopping days for as he went from shop to shop in High Street he had a leopard on a lead. The captain had a menagerie in his house near the Lock.

But he was best remembered for the firework displays arranged on Gossmore where the recreation ground now stands. The highlight and conclusion of each display was a set-piece. All it said was: 'Who ate puppy pie under Marlow Bridge?'.

BELOW LEFT: Thames Lawn, once Thames Bank House and later Lymbrook—once home of Admiral Morris, Commander of H.M.S. Colossus at Trafalgar.

BELOW RIGHT: Gifted amateur artist and 1964 UDC Chairman, the late Fred Butler was also pre-war Mayor of Henley.

ABOVE LEFT: Jerome K. Jerome lived in Marlow Common and wrote Three Men in a Boat. (Mansell Collection.)

ABOVE RIGHT: The delle Robbia frieze at Jerome's home—sculpted by Conrad Dressler.

BELOW: Jerome lived at Monks Corner.

BELOW RIGHT: George V visits Gyldernscroft.

115

LEFT: This drinking fountain commemorates US impresario
and Marlowphile Charles Frohman, drowned when
the Lusitania went down.

ABOVE RIGHT: John Richardson, Marlow-born showman.

BELOW RIGHT: Richardson's 'Piebald boy'.

ABOVE LEFT: Gen Sir George Higginson in ceremonial
robes—at St George's Chapel, Windsor.

ABOVE RIGHT: 1911 Marlow Corporation celebrations in trenchant style.

BELOW LEFT: Mrs Nesta Liston, Marlow's modern benefactress,
who gave the town Liston Hall and bequeathed New Court.

BELOW RIGHT: Carnival Parade in 1936.

Quarry Wood Hall in its Edwardian Gothic splendour—designed by Aubrey Beardsley, built in 1901, and rendezvous for the celebrities of yesteryear.

118

Players' Paradise

In the first half of the 19th century there was a racecourse at Marlow in the Riverwoods area, where Marlow Rugby Club have their present headquarters. It was an event that attracted the interest and support of the local gentry of the day—including at one time five Members of Parliament.

Usually held in August it was a two-day event dating from 1834. The first day's principal event was the Buckinghamshire Stakes—25 sovereigns each—and the Ladies' Purse of 20 sovereigns, added to a Sweepstake of five sovereigns each.

Leading owners of the day were interested in running their horses at Marlow, for there was a stipulation requiring previous winners of the Goodwood or Brighton Stakes to carry a 7lb. penalty, or 10lb. if they had won both events.

On the second day the main races were for a silver cup presented by Lieutenant Colonel Sir W. R. Clayton, Bart, MP valued at 20 guineas, added to a sweepstake of five sovereigns. The winner of this race had to be sold for 100 sovereigns if demanded. The other event was a hurdle race in which each horse had to carry 11st 4lb. and there were six jumps over four sets of hurdles. The winner was to be sold for 70 sovereigns.

On one of the posters dated 1835 there was an ominous footnote reading: 'All dogs seen on the course will be destroyed, and persons found damaging the Corn will be rigidly prosecuted'. No 'gambling devices' were allowed on the course.

In 1847 the Marlow Races went into decline. One of the main reasons was the withdrawal of the Clayton family patronage.

Yet Marlow has continued a sportsmen's paradise down the years, and in the last quarter of a century there has been an astonishing accent on recreation. At times the efforts to achieve facilities have reached fever pitch.

The Marlow area now has Court Garden leisure centre and swimming pool—less than a year old. And even today the Sports Council is bringing to completion a vast array of sports buildings and accommodation in the grounds of historic Bisham Abbey at an estimated cost of over four and a half million pounds.

But interest in sport is nothing new to the district and town. Today the area can be truly said to have maintained yet another of its many images—that of being a playground.

Of all local annual events, pride of place must go to the Marlow Amateur Regatta. Interest in boats, boating, to say nothing of punts and canoes, has been long-established.

The regatta was probably the first organised sports production arranged for the town, though its beginnings are shrouded in mystery. No proper records were kept until 1855. One of the posters advertising the regatta in that year exists to this day and is in the possession of the regatta committee as is one of the original trophies competed for—a beautifully worked silver oar.

Mixed fortunes and successes were the lot of the regatta after that small start until by 1870 its very future hung in the balance. Help was sought from Maidenhead. Assistance of a kind was forthcoming as a condition was made that the regatta should be held alternate years at Marlow and Maidenhead. This enforced co-operation brought a bad taste in its train, and finally in 1881 the arrangement disintegrated and no regatta was held.

Driven to near-distraction by this humiliation the regatta organisers called a public meeting in the Crown Hotel. As is almost always the case in Marlow when the chips are down, the population responded. The meeting decided to stage 'Great Marlow Regatta'. The word 'Great' referred to the town and not the event.

It was agreed the regatta of 1882 would take place on the Saturday following Henley Regatta, which in those days was a two-day event held on Thursday and Friday and, it is important to note, always the first Thames regatta of the season.

Duly in 1882 there was a programme of eight events and from the United States of America came the Hillside crew to take part in the Grand Eights—the first time an overseas entry was recorded. But there was a national dispute about the amateur status of the Americans, who were not allowed to enter Henley. All rowing organisations except Marlow Rowing Club boycotted the visitors. But in spite of Marlow's hospitality, the local oarsmen were easily defeated in the only competitive outing the men from the USA made.

The 1882 event set the regatta on the road to success, but locals clashed soon after about the manner in which the regatta was run. A strong lobby in 1895 deplored the conjunction of carnival and regatta.

The same people complained there was a 'lack of serious rowing'. Accordingly, 'Serious rowing' was given complete command of the regatta; the local rowing club agreed to take on the carnival. To this day the rowing club annually organise a 'Rag Regatta' in August, while the major rowing fixture takes place in June.

Marlow Amateur Regatta committee set about their task with new terms of reference and though they probably never spelled it out, it was their avowed intention to make the occasion world-famous.

Just how this eventually came about—for the event is world famous now—happened in a remarkable manner. In 1913, the Thames Amateur Rowing Council, which controls the allocation of regatta dates to Thames-based clubs, gave Marlow's traditional date of the second Saturday in August to Staines. Consternation in Marlow!

After weighing up the possibility of holding an August mid-week event, the Marlow men came up with an equally staggering answer. It was finally decided to hold Marlow Regatta on the third Saturday of June . . . two weeks before Henley! Consternation in the rowing world! It was unheard-of to hold a regatta before Henley, which traditionally started the season.

From that moment the reputation of Marlow Regatta increased until in the years immediately after the second world war it was fairly claimed to be the biggest one-day event of its kind in the world. Each year programmes have included over 100 races and invariably the final race in each year starts right on time.

Two men have dominated the history of the regatta: Alfred Davis and Charles Rowe. Both journalists working in Marlow, their combined connection with Marlow Regatta spanned 75 years. It was in 1892 that Alfred Davis was elected secretary, a position he held until his death in 1924. Charles Rowe, elected assistant secretary to Alfred Davis in 1912 took over in 1924 and remained secretary and treasurer until 1966 when he retired. He was elected President the following year for the remaining nine months of his life.

Marlow Rowing Club came into existence as the result of the persuasive influence of Colonel Tom Wethered. In the Spring of 1871 the club was formed.

Strange to relate, a great deal of support and sponsorship for the water-borne sportsmen came from the 'land-lubbers' at Marlow Football Club, who had been formed the previous year—also under the not inconsiderable influence of Colonel Tom Wethered, who was President of both clubs at the same time.

Highlight of the rowing club's existence was undoubtedly the winning for the United Kingdom of a Gold Medal in the Commonwealth Games of 1958. Michael Spracklen and Geoffrey Baker powered their way through all opposition in the Double Sculls event. But long before either of these modern gladiators were even thought of, Marlow Rowing Club had excelled. The two greatest crews ever to represent the club were the four of 1883-84 and the eight of 1913-14.

In 1971 the club celebrated its centenary year. To mark this occasion members decided to extend the accommodation at the Boathouse, on the Berkshire bank, in the shadow of Marlow Bridge. An appeal for £20,000 was launched.

The project doubled the amount of boat storage space and gave ample changing accommodation as well as a large area for social functions. The new section was officially opened in May 1975.

Marlow Football Club have an equally impressive record, though many of their achievements were in the 19th century. At that time they put together one of the best amateur teams in the country and when the FA Cup was mooted in 1871—just one year after the birth of the Marlow club—the locals were among the first 15 subscribers to the original trophy for the new competition.

Marlow did better than just help to pay for the Cup—they entered. Since the foundation of the English FA Cup—still the greatest national competition in the world—Marlow have never missed an entry. This is a record that can be equalled only by one other soccer club in Britain . . . near-neighbours Maidenhead United.

Then in 1881-82 season Marlow reached the semi-final of the Cup—even in the standards of those days, when there was a smaller entry than today, a staggering achievement.

And in 1892 Marlow was one of the 12 clubs elected to form the Southern League. They were elected with 24 votes, only three clubs receiving more—Chatham and Luton Town (26 each) and Millwall Athletic (25). Tottenham Hotspur received one vote only and were not elected!

Professionalism forced a withdrawal from the Southern League, and they became founder-members of the Spartan League in 1907. They withdrew from that competition soon afterwards and on the outbreak of the 1914-18 war were playing in Great Western Suburban League. Practically all the players rallied to the colours in the war so the club 'put up the shutters'.

During the war the old 'Crown' ground was sold to Mr Riley who formed a Trust Fund to preserve an open space there for ever. So the club played at 'Star Meadow' which was not enclosed. This was a field just off Wycombe Road and a stone's throw from the present Alfred Davis Memorial ground, opened in 1928.

Until the termination of the second world war Marlow had always prided itself upon being a soccer town. Sir William Borlase's School played soccer and it was from this source that a great many of the lads who donned the famous blue and white halves of Marlow learned the game.

But in 1947 about 40 young people met one cold, damp February evening in the Chequers

Hotel, in High Street. They decided to form Marlow Rugby Club. In the first full season, 1947-48, a fixture list for two fifteens was arranged. To begin with the club played on a field in Dedmere Road, changing at the rowing club premises, then entertaining the opposition at The Chequers Hotel.

The following year the club played on Alder Meadows, changing in a garage at the rear of the George and Dragon Hotel where tea was provided. Soon, though, Marlow Urban Council stepped in and offered the use of the cellars of Court Garden as changing rooms. These had been prepared as gas cleansing stations during the war. Ultimately, the Club settled at Riverwoods, site of Marlow Racecourse 120 years before.

Then Marlow Sports Club came into being on October 31, 1949. The Sports Club then consisted of three sections—Marlow Cricket Club; Marlow Hockey Club and Marlow Rugby Union Football Club.

In 1949 the directors of Thomas Wethered and Sons Limited, the brewery company, to whom the sports ground off Pound Lane belonged, decided to cut back on expenditure and the sports facilities at the Brewery were the first to feel the axe. The ground was offered to the town through the local council.

The Surveyor to Marlow Urban Council then was Kelvin Smith. He persuaded the brewery firm to lease the ground to a new body, to be known as Marlow Sports Club. He and Ken Drucquer became first joint secretaries of the club and to preserve the name in connection with the Brewery's ownership of the ground, Commander Owen F. M. Wethered became President. The then chairman of the urban council, Colonel H. P. Henderson, became the first chairman.

In 1950 a tennis section was formed. They played on grass courts but also wanted hard courts. Finally when the courts were laid in 1969 the cost was over £2,300. A Table Tennis section was added in 1960 and Marlow Boxing Club became a section four years later.

The tennis and table tennis sections were completely new ventures though the Marlow Boxing Club had been founded in 1955 by the late Alan McLachlan, a director of a local timber importing company.

But the Sports Club were not enjoying the best of financial health. In 1960 the sections were liberated. Having gained their independence the sections were then responsible for their own finances and the sports club as such became a central body of administration. The following year the club became a limited liability company. Since then it has demolished the old rugby club centre and built a new brick-built clubhouse adjacent to the old cricket pavilion.

The Marlow Cricket Club was formed in 1829, but on the outbreak of the first world war, lack of funds caused the sale of their ground, Messrs Thomas Wethered and Sons Limited purchasing it as a recreation ground for employees.

But the cricket club had been wound up in May, 1920, when it became obvious there were not going to be enough members to fulfil fixtures. Until 1950 the club was out of existence. In that year cricket interests revived.

The other major cricketing force in the town is Marlow Park Cricket Club. The 'Park' club started its existence as 'Marlow Working Men's Cricket Club'. Just exactly when it was formed is not clear but just after the turn of the century there were cricket matches on a flat piece of ground in the ownership of Lord and Lady Terrington on the north side of Henley Road. Later the club played its matches on Porter's Meadow near the Railway Station. Then before it finally moved to Higginson Park matches were played on Marlow Football Club ground. A subsidiary cricket club known as the 'Wednesday Club' played at

Higginson Park too, and there were stormy scenes between the two factions. Finally, members of the Wednesday Club persuaded Park members to share the cost of a professionally-laid cricket 'table'.

Like so many other clubs in the town they, 'Park', had yearned for 'a place of their own'. Marlow Council more than met them halfway and in 1960 Councillor Fred Butler, then chairman of the council, declared open the pavilion.

The Park club was only one of a number of sports bodies which had reason to be grateful to the local council. Apart from providing tennis courts, a putting green and maintaining the delightful open space of Higginson Park, the council granted a lease to Marlow Bowling Club and in their latter days began a development adjacent to Court Garden, the council headquarters.

The Marlow Bowling Club started life in the area at the rear of the Crown Hotel in Market Square, but once the Higginson Park Society was established they moved to their present green behind the walled garden. In 1972 the club celebrated their half-century of existence, and at that time were just coming to the end of one of the most remarkable records of any Buckinghamshire bowls club.

For in the years following the end of the second world war the Marlow club won the Bucks Cup 11 seasons, and included in that run a 'hat-trick' of victories in seasons 1968-69-70. In addition to these 11 wins they were runners-up on four occasions.

But the pinnacle of achievement by Marlow bowlers was in 1971. Three men, Ian Harvey, Arthur Plestedd and John Lewis won the English Bowling Association triples competition, then went on to become first holders of the British Isles triples title—the first occasion this contest was held.

John Lewis, who died in 1973, was also an England international at indoor bowls, though he was representing Desborough Club in that code of the game. The club produced three England trialists, J. W. Morton in 1938, his son George in 1950 and Ian Harvey in 1971. Harvey went on in the England Singles championship to the final in 1973 at Worthing, where he lost to David Bryant from Somerset, virtually world champion. In 1950 Don Harvey (no relation to Ian) and George Morton were runners-up in the England pairs.

At Bucks County level no club has a record to compare with Marlow. Apart from their domination of the Bucks Cup they were winners of the Benevolent Cup once and thrice runners-up; the Bucks triples trophy came to Marlow twice and they were runners-up five times; they won the pairs four times and were runners-up once; won the fours on four occasions and were runners-up once and in the County singles they produced three champions, Wally Griffin (1962), John Lewis (1966 and 1971) and Ian Harvey (1964, 1973 and 1974). Six times Marlow players were runners-up.

Like almost every other club in Marlow the bowlers strove for many years to get a 'place of their own'. Initially they shared a small wooden building with the Marlow Park cricketers within the precincts of the bowling green. Then about the same time that the Park club put up their new pavilion, the bowlers made their move, too.

Marlow Hockey Club was formed in 1907 and played on the Pound Lane Sports Ground. But the club, which was a founder-member section of Marlow Sports Club in October 1949, led a nomadic existence.

They left the Pound Lane ground to play on Gossmore for some seasons, and after a spell moved to Porter's Field near the Railway Station. Next came a move to that same flat area of ground owned by Lord and Lady Terrington at Spinfield Park, then on to Higginson Park. Finally they returned to Pound Lane in 1949 where they are currently based. There was no league hockey until two seasons ago and the club now participates in the Truman's South League.

Over the years a number of players have been supplied by Marlow to Bucks County teams, but probably the most prominent player ever to pull a Marlow shirt over his shoulders was Robin Laird. He eventually went on to captain Scotland.

The club itself has one claim to fame. Like Marlow Regatta, which claims to be the biggest one-day event of its kind in the world, the annual Marlow Hockey Festival, held on Easter Mondays, ranks as the largest one-day tournament of its kind in the British Isles.

Marlow Angling Club was born in 1937. Under the guiding influence of Fred Butler, the club made great strides. He was elected first chairman and he was re-elected annually until he died in 1970.

Over the years Marlow Club ran well but Archie Folley transformed their fortunes when he agreed to grant private water rights on the Marlow Reach to the club. The response in membership was astronomical. Eventually, the club committee fixed a ceiling of 500 on membership.

Marlow Sailing Club is yet another post-war organisation formed in 1967. The inaugural meeting took place at Marlow Rowing Club boathouse and since then the sailing club have been searching for a permanent base from which to operate. At present they have temporary facilities near Temple. Though there is no power-boat club in the area there are two water-ski clubs. This sport is comparatively modern and they are based on gravel pits that have been worked out along the floor of the valley from Marlow towards Little Marlow. At one time there was a grandiose plan to link all the gravel pits together and establish a 2,000 metres international class rowing course there, such as was eventually constructed at Holme Pierpoint in Nottinghamshire, but it fell through.

Probably the greatest step forward in the provision of sporting amenities in Marlow for a century came in September 1975 when after a hectic history, fraught with a great deal of local political in-fighting, the Sports Centre was officially opened by Councillor John Hester, chairman of Wycombe District Council.

Marlow Urban District Council were the creators of the idea to build a vast sports complex adjacent to Court Garden house, which housed the former council offices.

Background to this latest addition to Marlow's 'playground' facilities started in 1966 when Marlow Community Centre was formed. Marlow Council appeared to give backing to the project in principle in the early days and went so far as to earmark the site of the former house, The Rookery, for the proposed centre.

There was a long and involved history to the affair which culminated in the council withdrawing their promised financial support.

But the council by this time—around 1972—realised their life as an authority was running out. Under the local government re-organisation Marlow was doomed to a shotgun marriage with High Wycombe Borough Council and Wycombe Rural District Council.

There was all-round resentment, for the town of Marlow, if it ever had links with other towns in the area, always had a traditional antipathy to anything remotely connected with High Wycombe. It is probable there would have been less resentment if Marlow had been merged with Maidenhead and Windsor, but the die was cast in the faceless and remote burrows of Whitehall.

Having accepted the fact, the council then set about leaving the town of Marlow the best possible legacy. Plans were drawn up for the sports and leisure centre at Court Garden. The finance was to be provided from the sale of a number of other sites.

Shortly before plans were laid Mrs Nesta Liston, a town benefactor, died and left New Court, in a plum position in the town centre just off High Street, to the town for the benefit of Marlow people.

The house, standing in about four acres of ground, went to the council. They planned to build houses for elderly people in part of the grounds and sell off the portion nearest to High Street as a site for a commercial enterprise. Unhappily the price of land became depressed and the council was advised to stay their hand. When other pieces of land had been sold, it was considered safe to continue. So the new complex started.

One of the long-desired amenities in the town was a swimming pool. Major contributing factor to this was that in the late 1950s, schoolchildren were forbidden to swim in the Thames at the bathing place off Quarry Wood Road due to pollution. This meant that if children were to learn to swim they were faced with journeys to other towns.

Mrs Ruth Jewell, a member of the urban council for many years, and active in numerous other bodies, rode through the town streets on a carnival float when the local Round Table organised a parade of decorated vehicles in 1961 and the theme of her organisation's float was: 'We'll get that Pool, or my name's not "Jool".'

In 1974 the learner swimming pool was eventually completed next to the sports and leisure complex and the first person to swim a length was Mrs Jewell.

Three months later the new complex was opened. Another badly wanted amenity in the town was a large hall for drama productions, dinners and dances. Included in the centre is such a hall. The facilities include squash and badminton courts, bar facilities and a rifle range that can be used for an indoor cricket 'net'.

Marlow Rifle Club was formed before the 1914-18 war and reformed after the second world war. From 1921 to 1939 the club competed in both national and county league competitions. In the 1950s they used the Armoury, but when this was deemed not safe, they had to be content with a move to Maidenhead. Finally, the club was found new facilities at Court Garden.

The history of Court Garden house became closely linked with the town's great asset of Higginson Park when Mr Robert Griffin, who lived in the house, died in 1920.

As a result there was a distinct threat of the estate's fragmentation and sale in plots, for building riverside houses. Such a prospect appalled three prominent men in the town—Canon M. Graves, council chairman in 1921; L. J. Smith, chairman in 1934; and R. H. Cathcart. Entirely on their own initiative they started to raise money from private donors, with the objective of purchasing Court Garden and presenting it to the town.

After years of devoted work their efforts crystallised. On July 5, 1926, the title deeds of Higginson Park came into the possession of the town of Marlow. But before they did there had been a wonderful day of pageantry, the like of which the town has never seen since. General Sir George Higginson, a veteran of the Crimean War, and who later became aide-de-camp to Queen Victoria, celebrated his 100th birthday.

Princess Mary came to Marlow on that July day in the year of the General Strike. So did the Band of the Grenadier Guards, General Sir George's old regiment. The keys of Court Garden were presented to him by the Princess and General Sir George then handed them over to Marlow.

Marlow Race course.

Marlow Regatta 1902.

MARLOW RACES, 1840.

FIRST DAY, AUGUST 12TH.

The BUCKINGHAMSHIRE STAKES of 25 Sovereigns each, 15 ft. and only 5 if declared on or before the 20th of July. Three to remain in, or no Race. The Winner of the Goodwood or Brighton Stakes to carry 7lb. if both, 10lb. extra; twice round and a distance.

SUBSCRIBERS.

G. S. HARCOURT, Esq. M. P.	Mr. SMITH,	Sir G. NUGENT, Bart.
Sir E. CLAYTON-EAST, Bart.	Mr. T. THEOBALD	Colonel G. NUGENT
Sir W. R. CLAYTON, Bart. M. P.	Mr. CURWEN	G. BULKELEY, Esq.
G. C. DUPRE, Esq. M. P.	S. MACKAY, Esq. Jun.	Mr. S. DAY
Mr. S. SCOTT	J. SIMPSON, Esq.	Captain GARDNOR
Mr. J. WEBB	R. HAMMOND, Esq.	Earl of ORKNEY
Colonel A. HIGGINSON	W. PENN, Esq.	W. P. FREEMAN, Esq.
Mr. J. FRANKLIN	T. WETHERED, Esq.	Captain HAMILTON, M. P.
G. H. DASHWOOD, Esq. M. P.	C. S. MURRAY, Esq.	Mr. MAY
Viscount DRUMLANRIG	R. R. CLAYTON, Esq.	Mr. GARRARD

The LADIES' PURSE of 20 Sovereigns, added to a Sweepstakes of 5 Sovereigns each. Six Subscribers or no Race. Heats, twice round. To start at the Winning Stand; three yrs. old, 7st. 4lb. four, 8st. 8lb. five, 9st. six and aged, 9st. 4lb. Mares and Geldings allowed 3lb. Winners once in 1840 to carry 3lb. twice, 5lb. three times, 7lb. extra; Horses that have started three times and not won allowed 5lb. The Winner to be sold for 120 Sovereigns, if demanded, &c. Entrance, 10s. each, to go to the Fund.

SECOND DAY, AUGUST 13TH.

A SILVER CUP, (the gift of Lieut. Col. Sir W. R. CLAYTON, BART. M. P.) value 20 Guineas, added to a Sweepstakes of 5 Sovereigns each, for Horses of all ages. Heats, twice round. To start at the Winning Stand; three yrs. old, 7st. 4lb. four, 8st. 8lb. five, 9st. six and aged, 9st. 4lb. Mares and Geldings allowed 3lb. The Winner to be sold for 100 Sovereigns, if demanded, &c. Six Subscribers or no Race. Entrance, 10s. each, to go to the Fund.

A HURDLE RACE, of 5 Sovereigns each, with a Purse added. Heats, once round. To start from the Ditch-in, with six leaps over four sets of Hurdles. Horses to carry 11st. 4lb. each. The Winner to be sold for 70 Sovereigns, if demanded, &c. Entrance, one Sovereign each, to go to the Fund. Five Subscribers or no Race.

If any of the Stakes are walked over for, the public money will not be added. Winners of each Race to pay one Sovereign to the Racing Fund. Jockies to pay 5s. each for Weights and Scales, for each Race they ride; and all RIDERS to bring their Weights, and ride in proper Caps and Jackets. The COLOURS to be named at Entrance, or one Sovereign penalty for neglecting so to do.

Horses for the First Day's Races to be Entered at the CROWN INN, by Ten o'Clock on Wednesday Morning, August 12th; no Entrance will be taken after that time. Horses for the Second Day's Races to be Entered at the CROWN INN on Thursday Morning, August 13th, by Ten o'Clock; no Entrance will be taken after that time.

Half an Hour between each Heat, and no delay after the second Bell. To start each Day precisely at Two o'Clock.

Matches or Heats, to be run, on permission being first obtained of the Stewards; and all disputes to be decided by them, or whoever they may appoint, and their decision to be final. All Dogs seen on the Course will be destroyed; and persons damaging the Corn will be rigidly Prosecuted.

Application for Booth Standings to be made at the CROWN INN, on Saturday, August 8th, by Nine o'Clock. No Person to ride within the Lines, except the Riders for the Day's Racing, and the Officers of the Course, nor near the Horses when running.

∴ Subscriptions for next Year's Races will be opened each Day at the Winning Stand.

The RACE BALL will take place at the TOWN-HALL, on FRIDAY, AUGUST 14th.

Viscount DRUMLANRIG.
Lt. Col. Sir W. R. CLAYTON, Bart. M. P. } STEWARDS.

W. TYLER, Clerk of the Course, Marlow.

Marlow Races in 1840.

127

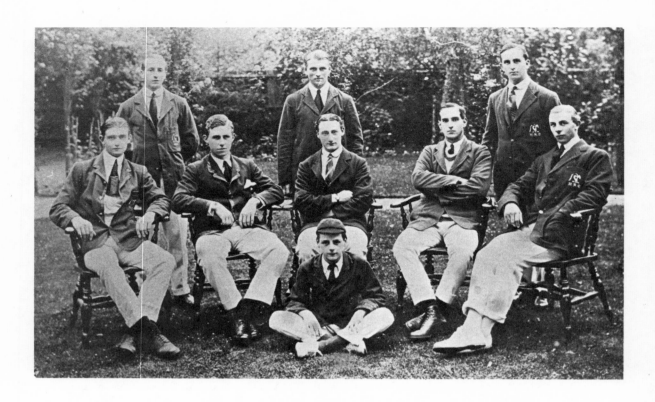

ABOVE: The great eight of 1913.

BELOW: The famous coxed four of 1883: left to right—W. T. Porter,
C. H. Yates, A. Shaw (Cox), J. S. Kirkpatrick, W. T. Shaw.

ABOVE LEFT: Marlow Rowing Club boathouse, 1901.

ABOVE RIGHT: Marlow RC boathouse today.

CENTRE: Michael Spracklen and Geoff Baker, Marlow's winners of the double sculls Gold Medal at the Commonwealth Games, 1958.

BELOW LEFT: Charles Rowe.

BELOW RIGHT: Alfred Davis.

ABOVE: Marlow FC 1881/2 team—FA Cup semi-finalists.

BELOW: 1970 reunion of Marlow FC past players,
with President Herbert Swadling and his wife.

ABOVE LEFT: Marlow Bowling Club's EBA triple champions—
left to right—John Lewis, Ian Harvey, Arthur Plestedd.

ABOVE RIGHT: Marlow Sports Club's new pavilion.

BELOW: Angling in 1920—seventeen years before
Marlow's club was formed.

131

ABOVE: The 1897 Jubilee Sports Committee.

CENTRE: Marlow Rifle Club between the wars.

BELOW: St Peter's Public Hall users in the early 1900s.

132

ABOVE: Great Marlow Institute: Jubilee Cricket Match in 1906.

BELOW: The Public Hall, once the Roman Catholic music
room, now the Marlow Masonic Centre.

133

ABOVE: Marlow's prize winning Town Band before the last war.

BELOW: Today's bandsmen (and women).

PUBLIC HALL
MARLOW.

MESSRS. EDGAR H. SCOTT & PERCY W FLINT
PRESENT

THE
MARLOW KOMEDY CONCERT KOMPANY

UP-TO-DATE
SONGS, SKETCHES
and DANCES etc.

IN THE ABOVE HALL ON
WEDNESDAY & THURSDAY, OCT. 6th & 7th, 1909
AT 8 O'CLOCK SHARP.

IN A REFINED AND UP-TO-DATE
DRAMATIC & MUSICAL PERFORMANCE
IN AID OF THE
MARLOW FOOTBALL CLUB

When the following Artistes will appear

Miss OLIVE STOOKE (Maidenhead Operatic Society)
Miss MARGARET CLISBY (1st Prize B.B & O. Festival)
EDGAR H. SCOTT (Principal London and Suburban Theatres)
FRED HARDS (Martin Harvey Dramatic Club)
And **Mr. TEDDY DRIVER** (Of the Principal London Halls. &c.)

ALSO THE FOLLOWING WELL-KNOWN ARTISTES

| T. U. DUNHAM | ARCHIE BURRETT | HARRY HAWKES |
| W. V. SLOAN | J. LANGLEY, Junr. | And PERCY FLINT AT THE PIANO) |

Concluding with a Sketch, entitled
'THE PHOTOGRAPHER'

ADMISSION - 2s. (Numbered & Reserved), 1s. & 6d. (limited)

Tickets to be obtained from members of the Football Club, Mr. W. DAVIS, High St; Mr. E. SCOTT, High St;
and Messrs. WELBOURNE & SIMPSON, The Library, High St.

WILLSONS NEW WALK COLOUR PRINTING WORKS LEICESTER

1909 Marlow concert poster.

ABOVE: Longridge, off Quarry Wood road—home to
the Boy Scout movement's national water sports.

BELOW: Harleyford Manor offers modern river-users
a marina and caravan facilities.

136

ABOVE: The Rookery, renamed Wrightlands, was to be
the Marlow Community Centre.

BELOW: Just across the river, a new sports complex rises
in the grounds of near neighbour Bisham Abbey.

ABOVE: Marly-le-Roi's Mairie or Town Hall—in 1973
just before the two towns were twinned.

BELOW: Marlow Chamber of Trade and Commerce gave this trophy to
their colleagues in France. (It was designed by the author—Ed.)

Great Marlow

As a community Marlow has never been subjected to dramatic and sudden progress. Changes have been made down the centuries in the appearance of the town and district, but these have rarely been achieved in haste.

The most sensational transition was when the town became a target for house buyers in the years immediately following the end of the second world war. And at the same time came the influx of industry, to give the town a taste of the second industrial revolution.

The hard core of Marlow people took it all in their stride, or most of it. When they saw something they did not like they were not slow to say so. Amenity societies were set up and they were listened to by authority.

The Thames still flowed by on its way to the sea; the frontage along the banks had been carefully preserved and in some cases improved; many derelict areas were transformed, and in the town itself many eyesores were removed and replaced by functional, easy-on-the-eye homes.

But then the cancer that had steadily been eating into commerce struck into the vitals of administration and there emerged the grand plan for bigger units. Commerce has since discovered to its cost that 'Big is anything but beautiful'.

Before the UDC expired, prominent citizens warned the amenity societies and commercial organisations of their importance, as the local touch went out of local government.

It can only be a matter of time before Marlow, until now a well-contained urban area, will erupt and spew out bricks and mortar as if from some volcanic crater into the surrounding area. And when the dust and smoke has settled, its status as an entity will have gone for good. So will that of Bovingdon Green, Seymour Plain and Marlow Bottom. Only the by-pass line will save Little Marlow from a similar fate, and Bisham may yet have cause to bless the Thames.

In recent years the town has stretched its hands across the sea in friendship to Continental neighbours and both French and German towns have reciprocated.

Before the United Kingdom entered into the European Economic Community partnership, Marlow was already making overtures to Marly-le-Roi, a town in a similar setting, near Paris.

A delegation from the French town 'twinned' with Marlow in 1972. Marlow went to Marly-le-Roi in the following year and tied the knot on French soil.

For eight years Marly had been twinned with a German town, Leichlingen, near Dusseldorf and Cologne. Marlow has embarked on a programme of completing the third leg of this international triangle.

Whatever happens to Marlow, the town, the spirit of the community will remain as it ever has, that of Great Marlow.

Clear indication of what lies round the corner for Marlow—
an aerial shot of Marlow, but a few yards from Seymour Plain,
and (opposite) . . . Bovingdon Green. (Aerofilms Ltd).

ABOVE : Signs of the times when earthmovers trample the countryside, this time to good effect, in clearing the by-pass route.

BELOW : One of Marlow's finest open spaces has spawned these prospective homes.

142

The Marlow that visitors admire, planners have
respected and that those who live here cherish.

143

Bibliography

A Short History of Marlow by J. C. Davies, 1962.

The History and Antiquities of the Hundred of Desborough and Deanery of Wycombe by Thomas Langley, 1797.

Magna Britannica by Rev Daniel Lysons, 1813.

The Thames from Source to Sea (Cassell & Company, Ltd, 1891).

The Marlow Rowing Club 1871-1921 by Alfred Davis, 1921.

Chiltern Country by H. J. Massingham, 1949.

Bucks Biographies by Margaret M. Verney, 1912.

Kelly's Directory for Buckinghamshire, 1888 and 1911.

Leland's Itinerary.

The Thames Highway by Fred S. Thacker.

Bucks Constabulary Centenary 1857–1957 by Alfred Hailstone.

History and Topography of the County of Buckinghamshire by James Joseph Sheahan, 1861.

History of Marlow Football Club, Charles W. Rowe, 1968.

A History of Borlase School, by J. C. Davies, 1932.

Bucks Archaeological Society Records 1861 to date.

Calendar to the Sessions Records; Vols I, II, III (Bucks County Council, 1933, 1936, 1939).

Victoria County History—Buckinghamshire, Vol III (1925).

Early Man in South Buckinghamshire by J. F. Head (John Wright & Sons, 1955).

Episcopal Visitation Book, for the Archdeaconry of Buckingham, 1662, ed E. R. C. Brinkworth (Bucks Record Society).

Ship Money Papers & Richard Grenville's Notebook, ed Carol G. Bonsey & J. G. Jenkins (Bucks Record Society).

Subsidy Roll for the County of Buckingham Anno 1524, ed Prof A. C. Chibnall & A. Vere Woodman (Bucks Record Society).

The Certificate of Musters for Buckinghamshire in 1522, ed Prof A. C. Chibnall (Bucks Record Society).

Political Change & Continuity 1760-1885—a Buckinghamshire Study by Richard W. Davis (David & Charles, 1972).

The Story of Sandhurst by Hugh Thomas (Hutchinson & Co Ltd, 1961).

Subscribers

Presentation copies

1 **MARLOW TOWN COUNCIL**
2 **Wycombe District Council**
3 **Buckinghamshire County Council**
4 **Marlow Branch Library**
5 **Cdr O. F. M. Wethered RN (Retd.), DL, JP**
6 **Brooke Furmston**
7 **Marly-le-Roi**

8 A. J. (Jock) Cairns	89 A. Moody	149 J. Deane
9 Clive Birch	90 Miss D. E. Talma	150 Diana & Bob Simpson
10 Alice Beard	91 Miss P. E. Wood	151 Gillian Petoud
11 Hugh A. Maddock	92 Dorothy Illingworth	152 Denis Combes Butt
12 Mrs H. E. Browne	93 P. W. F. Kingsbury	153 The Rev & Mrs
13 W/Cdr J. A. P. Owen	94 Miss M. F. Fuller	David A. Smith
14 P. E. Williams	95 C. Baker	154 Mr & Mrs M. Burke
15 Mrs T. Henley Coulson	96 Jack Connelly	155 D. N. Vidgen
16 Dr P. A. Diplock	97 Mrs J. Isemonger	156 D. M. McQueen
17 Mrs G. I. Bettle	98 J. R. C. Ellis	157 E. G. & C. G. Silvey
18 Mr & Mrs Michael Post	99 David Wheeler	158 Mrs M. Allen
19 P. Barker	100 L. W. G. Oxley	159 J. G. Laurence
20 Mrs P. E. Teasdill	101 R. Jenks	160 Cynthia & Laurie
21 J. Morrison	102 Miss S. Kempson	Ewins
22 C. Calcutt	103 W. McKnight	161 J. A. Cooper
23 J. H. Lowe	104 } Henry Clayton	162 T. W. Stokes
24 G. J. White	105 }	163 D. P. Vickers
25 A. Tarry	106 D. B. McLean	164 Mrs J. Walker
26 Tom Walsh	107 Mrs P. Coward	165 Janet, Sophie & Michael
27 Jean Bray	108 L. R. Stroud	New
28 Mrs Drewett	109 Mr & Mrs C. W.	166 Mr & Mrs A. R.
29 Mrs D. Dickson	Fordham	Arnold
30 Geoffrey Moss	110 E. H. Sendall	167 G. A. H. Williams
31 H. M. Bazeley	111 Mr & Mrs R. G.	168 Peter Swadling
32 Anne Paling	Batting	169 Mr & Mrs E. S. Reeve
33 D. G. Dean	112 Mrs C. L. Harvey	170 Mrs Frances Riches
34 J. Evans	113 R. Whiting	171 Mrs Daisy M. Walker
35 D. W. North	114 J. M. & D. J. Manchip	172 Christine Hains
36 Mrs Barbara Browne	115 C. A. Hill	173 J. E. Price
37 A. H. Child	116 A. Jenkins	174 B. J. Buttle
38 Mrs C. Lee	117 M. R. Child	175 J. K. Dixon
39 Mrs Hilary Walker	118 G. L. Currell	176 Mrs M. V. Ojjeh
40 R. J. Kemp	119 P. T. Plumridge	177 R. A. & E. J. Fowler
41 Mrs N. Andrews	120 Mrs P. M. Henderson	178 Mr & Mrs E. L. Nicholl
42 Mrs K. O. Reed	121 R. C. Warner	179 Miss J. T. Walker
43 Mrs J. E. Chown	122 Mrs M. Ashworth	180 Clive Sanders
44 Mrs R. Payne	123 D. M. Walker	181 M. Tucker
45 Mrs Sendall	124 R. W. Mogg	182 R. Johnson
46 John R. King	125 J. O. Denton	183 John H. Evans
47 W. Howard Phillips	126 Joan & Bill Streeter	184 Mrs P. Langley
48 Mrs A. E. Brench	127 T. G. & K. M. Sutcliffe	185 Mrs G. Tubb
49 D. Ellis	128 Ron & Ray Woodward	186 Terry & Enid Lloyd
50 Mrs Nova Williams	129 C. L. & J. M. Chappell	187 Mrs A. Lewis
51 Mrs Gerald Russell	130 M. Scarles	188 Dr Helen R. B. Brown
52 Stanley Wagstaffe	131 Anthony Hinds	189 Miss M. Mackenzie
53 Mrs V. E. I. Lee	132 Mr & Mrs B. P. White	190 R. M. Hodges
54 Joy E. Newman	133 Hugh McNearnie	191 Major Douglas F. Pluck
55 Mrs Y. Cook	134 S. H. J. Card	FRICS
56 K. J. Fry	135 Mrs M. Price	192 Mrs D. W. Shipp
57 Mrs M. Child	136 Mrs M. M. Johns	193 Mr & Mrs Derek B.
58 Mrs O. Eldridge	137 C. Mifsud	Woolford
59 M. G. Holland	138 S. M. Purser	194 A. Johnston
60 F. H. N. Layton	139 A. F. Gray	195 Miss C. M. Chalmers
61 Miss J. C. Webb	140 Mrs J. H. Turner	196 P. J. Allen
62 Stewart Spencer	141 Mrs Myra Faulkner	197 Mrs E. M. Turner
63 Simon Oliver Murphy	142 Col J. Pounds	198 R. Gladman
64 R. C. Brant	143 Hilda Coster	199 Mrs Adamson
65 S. A. Beaver	144 R. A. Gillman	200 Ron & Jacqueline
66 Mrs G. L. Gwynnett	145 Mr & Mrs C. G. H.	Tempest-Woods
67 V. A. Rouse	Perry	201 I. H. Spanton
68 Mrs W. E. Johnson	146 Mr & Mrs A. S. Evans	202 Miss M. Griffin
69 Mrs J. Brooks	147 Mrs Ansell	203 Mr Barnes
70 Robert Wright	148 Mr & Mrs D. Heritage	204 Mrs E. L. Spencer
71 A. G. Hopwood		
72 M. Beaver		
73 Michael V. V. Leggate		
74 Mrs A. M. de C. Wright		
75 R. G. Lock		
76 Peter Badge		
77 W. H. J. Smith		
78 Martha R. Partridge		
79 E. F. J. Smith		
80 Mrs A. S. H. Evans		
81 Mrs V. J. Beadle		
82 } Mrs M. T. H. Cox		
83 }		
84 R. A. Boult		
85 Donald J. Nicol		
86 Yvonne E. Steer		
87 Mrs Jean Mackrill		
88 Jean Collins		

205 R. B. Jenkins
206 John R. C. Boys
207 M. R. Cary
208 Joanna Brown
209 Capt J. B. McEwen
210 Dr E. L. Leafe
211 Mrs K. J. Goodway
212 F. E. Ridley
213 G. A. Carter
214 John K. Davies
215 Mrs M. Fenton
216 S. T. Jackson
217 G. H. R. Meakes
218 N. R. Levins
219 D. P. Blow
220 D. J. Browne
221 Mrs C. M. Fountain
222 A. Jones
223 Miss M. W. Eddowes
224 Mrs C. Deverall
225 Mrs A. G. Lee
226 Foxes Piece County Middle School
227 Mrs C. James
228 Miss Sarah Pothecary
229 D. W. Jones
230 Sqn Ldr J. D. Crier
231 B. H. Rockell
232 A. Rockell
233 Mrs Heller
234 Mrs E. M. Hayter
235 Mrs G. Brookman
236 K. D. Spivey
237 D. E. Boyt
238 S. F. Hillsdon
239 J. Penney
240 J. F. Day
241 Mrs J. I. Fulcher
242 Mrs M. Bullen
243 C. J. Baker
244 E. M. Baker
245 P. Stilwell
246 Ray Maskery
247 G. L. Dean
248 Ian Loudon Brown
249 R. G. Batting
250 J. N. Shine
251 Mr & Mrs R. Brownjohn
252 Miss D. K. Millington
253 M. C. Brown
254 Miss D. E. M. McCall
255 Conal P. O'Sullivan
256 G. H. Palmer
257 Mrs Rita Price
258 S. J. Harbord
259 Mrs E. M. Maidment
260 F. G. Brown
261 D. G. Veale
262 J. W. Dexter
263 C. T. Kyte
264 P. White
265 Trevor Saint
266 Mrs J. Price
267 Mrs J. V. Fontannaz
268 M. Howard
269 Roy Fox
270 V. J. Vassall-Adams
271 Mrs C. M. Birchall
272 R. J. E. Platt
273 David Sumpter
274 J. F. Brindley
275 Mrs A. M. Walker
276 J. Blanco-Vazquez
277 J. Meeks
278 A. T. Owen
279 F. R. Morgan
280 Mrs B. Shephard
281 Mrs I. M. Lee
282 Thelma E. Vernon
283 R. A. Brewster

284	D. H. Head	334	Mrs B. M. Johnson	382	M. J. B. Taylor	439	H. Ward
285	E. R. Davies	335	} Mrs C. Harding	383	G. Shipp	440	Eric G. Silvey
286	Eric F. Burger	336	}	384	I. R. Gould	441	R. F. A. Freeman
287	Alan Holmes	337	A. C. Frost & Co	385	Mrs J. I. Smith	442	Mr & Mrs R. Kelly
288	} A. J. Cairns	338	R. R. Faul	386	Mr & Mrs Bernard L. Wells	443	} Mrs A. Hufflett
290	}	339	Brenner Brenchley	387	Ann Allen	445	}
291	Douglas Brown	340	F. G. Wigmore	388	B. P. Collins & Co	446	R. B. Hook
292	Isla Wootton	341	} Keith Chamberlain	389	D. E. Tracey	447	F. K. Clarke
293	K. Balfour	342	}	390	A. W. Devereux	448	Mr Newcombe
294	A. Boarder	343	Mrs Y. Smith	391	Mr & Mrs R. J. Fagg	449	Dr T. C. Williams
295	V. J. Boveington	344	D. Clark	392	Mrs M. J. Wilkinson	450	} D. J. Rockell
296	D. A. Atherton	345	O. B. Gilbart-Smith	393	N. Pollitt	451	}
297	Arthur Tomlinson	346	Mrs B. H. Janes	394	Mrs C. M. Davis	452	Mrs Jacqueline Miles
298	Miss Peggy Rose Ives	347	Mrs Jane Canning	395	W. J. H. Humphries	453	Geoff Thomas
299	Mrs K. G. Leigh	348	Jenny Cadet	396	Mrs D. Lyne	454	} R. A. Campbell
300	Mrs E. M. Mitchell	349	E. J. Jordan	397	D. A. Coster	455	}
301	J. S. Paine	350	G. H. Davis	398	Mrs B. Ayres	456	Raymond W. Birch CBE
302	Mrs H. Lovesey	351	G. W. Hughes	399	J. G. Laing	457	Mrs M. D. Boyden
303	P. C. Nunn	352	P. Cambell	400	Dr Richard J. Marsh	458	A. E. Vere
304	H. W. Hall	353	Mrs R. M. Green	401	H. C. Lunnon	459	Stephen & Vicki Wegg Prosser
305	Mrs V. Nicholls	354	J. D. Weir	402	Louella Eva	460	Malcolm Read
306	Mrs R. J. Field	355	Mrs A. Platt	403	Mrs B. Chapman	461	David Read
307	Robert E. Ticehurst	356	Mr & Mrs H. B. Grice	404	M. Harpin	462	F. R. Smith
308	G. J. Edwards	357	G. G. Davies	405	D. J. Scroggins	463	Peter Chard
309	} Cdr O. F. M.	358	H. J. Cryer	406	Mrs M. E. Mulady	464	Valerie C. Baskwill
311	} Wethered RN	359	J. P. Asplin	407	Derek A. Lessware	465	Dr G. H. Wyatt
312	Jack Lennard	360	R. R. Brereton	408	David Hodges	466	Mrs Mary Cowling
313	M. Glover	361	K. Emery	409	G. J. Bustin	467	H. L. Jameson
314	C. T. Stevens	362	Mrs M. E. Watson	410	G. G. James	468	R. M. Kimber
315	Percy James Allen	363	Mrs J. Addis	411	Ronald Levin	469	C. Gibbons
316	E. M. Page	364	Mrs A. D. McNair	412	A. Richardson	470	D. Perry
317	B. G. Child	365	W. D. Hodgson	413	} Bucks County Library	471	C. R. Folley
318	David Lynch	366	H. W. Cross	424	}	472	J. D. S. Hester
319	R. Price	367	Sir John Hall, OBE, MP	425	Mrs B. M. Taylor	473	A. D. Mills
320	Mrs C. H. Moore	368	Geo. E. Marsland	426	Mrs B. Ennis	474	Mr & Mrs M. J. Clark
321	Dr Anne Cooper	369	Ruth V. Jewell JP	427	Mrs A. M. Foster	475	Mr & Mrs D. F. Hamilton
322	Patrick Cavendish	370	M. H. Dorsett	428	Dr R. F. Packham	476	G. D. Thomas
323	Robert J. Mitson	371	Mrs W. M. Dix	429	Mrs R. D. Arnott	477	Mrs V. Cheesman
324	G. H. Wyatt	372	P. C. Richardson	430	Rev William Fillery	478	Mrs E. A. B. Orr
325	J. R. Alcock	373	Ultra Electronics Ltd	431	Mrs C. Goff	479	A. D. Clark
326	Mr & Mrs S. McCabe	374	Mrs H. Tarry	432	Philippe A. Burger	480	D. K. Hampton
327	Mrs E. Annable	375	Mrs M. J. Carvey	433	S. J. Cook	481	N. W. Deane
328	Mrs R. Annable	376	Mr & Mrs D. W. Bodey	434	A. C. Fyvie		
329	Jack L. P. Vere	377	G. C. L. Mason	435	F. Terry		Remaining names unlisted
330	J. P. Luckett	378	H. Woodward	436	Ann Spracklen		
331	William A. Anderson	379	R. Pearson	437	Maureen Sherry		
332	R. W. Stanley	380	} Miss G. O. Hughes	438	M. W. Puzey		
333	T. A. Jones	381	}				

Index

147

ENDPAPERS: FRONT: 'Temple and Harleford', drawn in 1793 by
J. Farington, RA and engraved by J. C. Stadler.

BACK: High Street, Marlow, from a 19th century sketch.